ULTIMATE COMMUNICATION SECRETS

CREATE AUTOMATIC SUCCESS

ULTIMATE COMMUNICATION SECRETS

CREATE AUTOMATIC SUCCESS

HAMESH C YADAV

White Falcon Publishing

www.whitefalconpublishing.com

Ultimate Communication Secrets
Hamesh C Yadav

www.whitefalconpublishing.com

In collaboration with

Want Solution
www.wantsolution.com

ISBN - 978-93-88459-38-9

❊ Contents ❊

A Note to The Reader

This short, wisdom rich, and crisply written book couldn't be more well-timed. Never have we had such an abundance of resources, information, freedom, choices and tools to better our lives, yet we are facing an epidemic of mental disorders. According to World Health Organization *'by 2030 depression will be the leading cause of disease burden globally'*. I believe one of the leading cause of the decline in our mental health and well-being is our lack of understanding and ability to use our mind *aka* train our mind to better our lives. Most of the people today are working extremely hard to bring about success and overcome challenges in their life. But they are only tapping into the 10% of their minds capacity. Your chances of success in any given area of your life depends upon your ability to tap into and change the dormant 90% (Subconscious) mind. Unless you learn how to rewire and reprogram your subconscious mind, success in your life will feel like taking 2 steps forward and 3 steps back. Life will feel like a treacherous journey!

In this book, Hamesh carefully and thoughtfully shows how you can be the master of your destiny and achieve extraordinary results in the areas of your health, wealth, parenting and relationships. This book will act as your personal workbook for the Journey of Self-Discovery, and will enable you to gain greater control over your thoughts, words, emotions, behaviours and results in your life.

There are many ways to approach a book of this kind. One way would be to plunge directly into practices, to take a deep dive into the wisdom and overcome your limitations. Other way would be to use it as a manual to deepen your understanding about human behaviour and emotions, and embark upon the journey of Self-Mastery. The journey that can be made by no one, but you.

This book will provide you, with the maps to the terrain and offer you the ways to navigate it. It is not a display of his academic expertise. Instead, he seeks to offer series of fundamental insights- that will help you lay a strong foundation for what he likes to call- "Automatic Success"- in every area of life. They are core perspectives that have emerged because of over 20 years of his experience of working in the East and West in human behaviour.

Hamesh is not offering you anything new but – 'what is true'. He is not interested in giving you the Band-Aids, dealing with the symptoms, but in educating you. He has given simple but immensely powerful tools to eradicate the root cause of the problem.

I met Hamesh, 5 years ago at a business development seminar. During our interaction, I was mesmerized by his understanding of human behaviour and his approach toward handling life challenges and goals. Since then, we have regularly stayed in touch. I am impressed by his desire to constantly learn from the best sources and transform the lives of people who cross paths with him.

As you go through this book, there will be several instances you will be struck with the insights- Insights from a place of clarity. It will reveal to you the patterns, that keep you limited or stuck, patterns that bring you success, patterns that make you sad or depressed or anxious, and patterns that bring you Peace, Joy & Happiness.

If knowledge is power, then knowledge about self will help you become Empowered, and ultimately attain Self-Mastery.

May You Live a Magnificent Life & Uplift Countless Others In Your Lifetime
Enjoy!

Harish Gulati
Success Coach, Founder of Empowered Thinking Academy
Best Selling International Author
'Think Before You Think'
Bestselling Instructor at Udemy

Testimonials

"In my last few coaching sessions, **Hamesh** gave me a level of self-awareness that took me to another level with my personal goals and develop a leadership mentality and be able to guide other people to realise their goals.

We started using Hamesh's services few years back and attended his workshops on Professional Growth and mindsets. Our staff derived infinite advantages both in terms of personal and professional growth and development to un-tap the hidden power of professional growth model by understanding the pattern of people and organization behaviour.

From the first time we worked with **Hamesh,** he made us feel so comfortable. His genuine and fun approach as well as ability to connect with our situation whilst giving us great insight was simply amazing. He understands what his clients need and delivers in the most engaging way that gets results on a long-term basis. *I highly recommend Hamesh as an excellent Life Coach.*"

Kawalpreet Singh CPA (CEO – Integrated Accountants)

I am doing a big thank you shout out to **Hamesh Yadav.**

We had a coaching session around my WHY. As we started, I felt at ease and relaxed and what I truly got to see was my resistances and blocks around my Why and how they had been impacting my life!

We then identified that it was related to unresolved experiences from my childhood.

I had a distinct experience of feeling in my body a young part of me that had been hurt, didn't trust or feel safe.

Hamesh then facilitated working with my inner child and re-integrating the 4yr old Ben, back into myself to where that young Ben does feel held and feels safe.

People have asked me to recall what the feelings of that inner child were. The best part is I can't, now that it has been re-integrated it is done and complete, for that, I am very thankful. 😊

Hamesh went above and beyond, he gave me the time needed for the process to happen.

I am very grateful that this process has been done and now have space for new possibilities in my life.

I would definitely recommend Hamesh to anyone who is coming up against blocks and wants to create new possibilities in their life.

Thank you. Ben Komo, Life coach and
Energy Healer. Melbourne 😊

My name is Sowji, a full-time businesswoman.

I started taking Hamesh Yadav 's consultation in March this year.

I was suffering from anxiety and ego related problems which are entirely unknown to my notice.

Once I went through the counselling, I was stunned with his observations and valuable suggestions.

Before attending the consultation, I was very easily triggered by others words and very impatient. I was having issues in our relationship with my husband due to my ego which even I was unaware of.

Before the consultation, I was so frustrated because I could not figure out what is the actual reason that is causing all the problems.

In a few sessions, he figured out the whole problem lies in my behaviour and the way I am looking at things.

I went through the sessions I loved the way Hamesh Yadav handled the problem, and the solution provided changed my life and the way I look at life.

I experienced many changes in my life just not for myself but for my family as well.

I strongly recommend Hamesh Yadav for your better relations in life.

Sowji Nekkalapudi.
Entrepreneur, Mother and wife.

Hey Hamesh,

Thanks for spending time with me the other day.

I was impressed with your command on the key drivers of our psychological tendencies and understanding of self-limiting human behaviour.

Once again, thank you for taking the time out and having a discussion with me.

Cheers!

Bill.T
Former Teacher

I Learned from Hamesh, How to build positive relationship between couple and how to lead good family life.

Jayaprakash Nekkakpudi.
Commissioning supervisor
Honeywell, Melbourne

How unconscious mind works and what are the impact of this in our day-to-day life and how our verbal and non verbal communication style impact on whole process, pay attention on non-verbal one.

Vijay Konepepndi.
I.T Expert

Hamesh help me to learn how to come out of the comfort zone and take the opportunity all opportunity that are available with thinking positive and with growth mindset.

Prathyusha
Accountant, Melbourne

I work as a Senior Project Manager at Public Transport Victoria. Last year I got in touch with Hamesh Yadav to get his guidance on few of the my personal challenges. Before meeting him, I have already tried couple of counsellors but there was no improvement. After meeting him I felt an instant connection as he could understand me as person and provide me valuable suggestions which changed my life for ever. My life has not got a proper direction and my relationship with my family members and at work place and with my friends has improved drastically.

Ashish Khurana
Senior Project Manager, Program Delivery
(Business & Systems Projects)
Network Integrity, Projects and Assurance

Hi my name is Amit Verma. I work as a manager in a transport company and also founder of Moorabbin kebab and burger. I started using hamesh services since last year. I have attended his workshops on art of relationship and key to success. Since I have started using his services there have been significant improvements in my work and relationships with my family and community. Hamesh is a person with huge experience and knowledge. I highly recommend all of you if you are struggling in any field and need expert advice, look no far and get in touch with Hamesh.

Amit Verma
Manger and Entrepreneur
Melbourne

I am a Fleet leasing officer and also an Independent Business Owner

I started using Hamesh ji's services almost 1 year ago. And I am glad that I made that decision for myself. When Hamesh ji, explained me about the coaching and mentoring he does, I wasn't sure if I really wanted to do it but yes the confidence he gave me in lending his ears made me signing up the Happy agreement with him and my journey began.

Going back to myself and seeing what I was 12 months back, I see a female, who was frustrated, upset, lacked energy and had started to loose the self confidence. But things changed.....changed for good. I learnt so much in this one year journey that I can't even pen down all but just to name a few, learnt to be positive or I must say learnt to see positive in the negative too, learnt to have different perspectives, different approach and thought process.

Hamesh ji went through an entire brain system from A-Z on how to present myself powerfully. How to use affirmations? He made me think of the, "Why", that why someone is doing this to you. He made me think of the possible reasons which eventually changed me and my thought process. Therefore, rather than being upset on the person who did the wrong thing it now changed to why did this even happen. It has been a complete shift in my behaviour.

What Hamesh ji offers, is a tailor suited package. He talks and switches as per the mood of the other person and picks it up from there. And starts to coach and mentor the mood and fits a whole new thought process in your head.

I am really blessed to have his support in my life and do give him credit as now I am more confident, I understand situations better and react maturely. That happy agreement has binded me with it and I see happiness and positivity.

In the gist, I would like to thank Hamesh ji for his continuous support and playing such an important role of changing lives of the people. I am certain there are many more waiting for you out there!!!

Thanks & Regards,
Sakshi Datta
McMillian Shakespeare Group

Introduction

Aisee Vani Boliye, Maan Ka Aapa Khoye
Apna Tan Sheetal Kare, Auran Ko Sukh Hoye

Translation 1
Speak such words, you lose the mind's Ego
One's Body remains composed, Others Find Peace

Translation 2
Speak such words, sans ego's ploy
One's Body remains composed, giving the listener joy

Meaning
In speech, use such words that your ego is eliminated. Don't brag, don't gloat, and don't make yourself out to be big, important, rich or anything else that the ego attaches to.

Building the Ego takes energy away from the body, and takes away the body's composure. If ego is lost in one's speech, the listener finds peace from listening to it.

My Understanding
This Doha (a type of poetry in India) is a gem. It deals with human psychology, metaphysics, and a basic tenet of the Indian philosophy. The ancients of the Vedic literature have laid tremendous emphasis on speech.

Do you know that our speech has a direct connection with our bodily humors? It is proclaimed that sound and sight are the underlying sources of all vibrations.

This has been scientifically proven over and over again. Spoken words, human speech, flow exclusively from the exhalation of the breath. While inhaling, one cannot speak. Thus the *Pranava,* or the breathing system itself, makes speech a process of the outgoing phenomenon.

Words once spoken cannot be retrieved

Hence, instead of being apologetic or remorseful later on, it is better to maintain the proper checks and balances on one's speech.

We know that all sounds create vibrations. And these vibrations affect both the speaker and the listener. Soothing, compassionate, and loving words breed togetherness, while harsh speech breeds hatred. And, we also know that human speech is one of the main ingredients that differentiate mankind from the rest of the animal kingdom.

Thus, with the above perspective, we can deduce that Kabir, in this Doha, crystallizes the power of the spoken word. He teaches us to speak in such a manner that keeps us harmonious and composed thereby making the listener feel a sense of joy in the communication.

I am sure that you have heard about the subconscious mind. You can find and read hundreds of books on this topic and how to use the power of your subconscious mind. I am not going to mention any particular book here, but it was my curiosity about the subconscious mind that led me to discover that there are hundreds of books out there on this topic.

Most of them are about how to attract money, a desirable partner, lose weight, and so on. But so far, I haven't found any book which tells you how to build or develop your subconscious mind. I am keenly interested in learning and sharing with you how we can build our subconscious minds and, by doing so, how we can change our reactions.

Purpose

I have observed that lots of grown adults face challenges in their day-to-day lives. This is totally normal, but my main concern is the baggage from their problems which they carry all the time. This is the unaddressed emotional effect of those problems. Most of the time, they don't even know where they collect all this stuff which is really bothering them.

As you probably know, 90% of our brain is controlled by our subconscious mind and only 10% is controlled by the conscious mind. My main focus is helping you learn how to develop the other 90% of your mind.

First, we will examine where the roots of the subconscious mind can be found. If something is really creating problems in our life, we must fix that, but the question is how. Before we can fix the problem, we must know where the problem lies and how it came into existence.

Just as when we visit a doctor and the doctor asks us many questions before prescribing a medicine, the reason why he asks so many questions is that he must make a diagnosis. Before he can make a diagnosis, he must know the signs and symptoms of the disease or disorder so that he can prescribe the right medicine in order to cure the disease. This is one part of fixing the problems.

However, everyone knows prevention is better than cure. Those people carrying their emotional baggage need help to prevent the problem from starting in the first place.

There are various important exercises throughout this book. Each of the exercise will help you learn and apply the tools to your circumstances.

To make it easier I have also compiled them into one convenient, well organized workbook. You can download and print this workbook for free.

Additionally I have created an online course to help you understand communication styles of different personality types. To get the most out of this book, I highly recommend that you enroll yourself in the online course now because it's one more gift I created just for you.

www.royallifecoaching.com
Please use code UCS2014

Chapter 1

❖ Developing the Growth Mindset ❖

"Creative energy surges through me and leads me to new and brilliant ideas."

We need to focus on communication because the gap is getting bigger and wider, especially in the coming generation who love to play on electronic devices and even communicate through these devices as well. I have seen lots of parents frustrated with this behavior of their kids. The parents also notice that if someone texts them (their kids) they reply, but a call... no way they are going to pick it up.

Such conduct gives certain indication of the kids' behavior and leads others to ask a few questions like:

Why he/she is avoiding the calls? Maybe he/she is sick and tired. If this happens only sometimes, it's ok; but if this is a regular practice, it means we need to dig in a little more. There may be some kind of fear or an underlying problem which we may need to investigate further and find out. It could even be a fear of not being good enough.

Everywhere you go, you hear people talking about mindset. Most of the successful people say that the psychology of a person plays a vital role in the outcome of their lives. Tony Robbins says 80% of success is resourcefulness and only 20% is mechanics.

Laura A. Jana, M.D. says, the toddler brain builds a habit at an early age.

Most of the successful people say: Psychology of a person plays a vital role in their life. Tony Robbins says 80 percent of this is resourcefulness and 20 percent is mechanics. Wherever you go, everyone talk about mindset.

What is mindset?
Your mindset is made up of many different things.

Beliefs: First is your beliefs, which is how you have built your subconscious mind, and how it works for you. According to Laura A. Jana, M.D., the toddler's brain begins building beliefs and habits at a very early age.

The belief of needing to be perfect is one the causes why people suffer a lot. It leads to superiority and inferiority complexes. My professor used to say that there is no superiority complex, just inferiority complexes.

Values: Values are another part of your mindset. This is how you value yourself and on what basis things get added to your priority list. What governs your life, or as Tony Robbins would say, who is driving your bus. You can have shadow values, which are values that you hold and you aren't even aware are there.

Confidence: This is another factor in your mindset. It determines how you build and how it helps you.

Whenever I asked questions in school, in place of giving me answers, teachers made fun of me or said, "Put your hand down." This stopped my curiosity and led me to stop asking questions. I lost confidence in myself because of this.

Standards are part of your mindset, too. They define your lifestyle, decision making, and confidence. These are taught at an early age.

Your **identity** determines how you see yourself and what you must do to maintain that image. Your happiness comes from how you define it and what you do to get it.

Your **ego** is a very important part of your mindset. It is the part of the mind that mediates between your conscious and subconscious mind. It is responsible for your sense of personal identity and for testing new ideas to see if they fit with your beliefs.

Your **ability to trust others** is another part of your mindset. It determines how easy it is for you to work with, and get along with, other people.

Yet another part of your mindset is **Discipline.** Many people procrastinate on tasks they know they need to do, and thus they don't end up succeeding in life as they would like to. Discipline is a habit formed at an early age. It teaches the mind to prioritize tasks and finish them as early as possible rather than postponing them.

The habit of **procrastination** can be developed either because you were getting positive reinforcement for getting tasks done at the last moment, or you were not checked and corrected. It can be defined as doing only those things where we get immediate gratification.

An example of the need to develop a habit of discipline is the marshmallow experiment. In the 1960's-1970's, students at Stanford University conducted an experiment on young children. They were given one small marshmallow if they took it right away or two somewhat larger ones if they were able to wait 15 minutes.

The **ability to wait longer** to get a better reward was shown to be predictive of a better life, outcome over time, as revealed by SAT scores, educational outcomes, body mass index (BMI), and other factors.

Resourceful Thinking, Communication, and Language

Most people think self-esteem means feeling good about yourself.

Self-esteem can never be implanted by the comments of others. It can be interfered with by an excess of criticism or unearned praise.

Communication is the key to resourceful thinking. We need to focus on it because the gap between people is getting wider and wider, especially in the coming generations.

They love to play on and communicate using their electronic devices. I have seen a lot of parents who are frustrated by this behavior of their children. The children say if someone texts them, they reply, but they won't respond to a phone call.

When we see such tendencies in our kids we need to ask a few questions. Why is our child avoiding phone calls? It may be that they are sick and tired of the phone. If that happens only sometimes, it's okay, but if it becomes a regular practice, we need to dig a little deeper. There may be some kind of fear, possibly a fear of not being good enough, and we need to find it out.

At times they are just modeling the behavior they see in their parents, like when parents keep checking their devices rather than paying attention to their children. I'll take my own example here.

My son and I were playing together when he was 2 years and 8 months old. My mobile phone buzzed with the sound of a text. I picked it up to have a look and he saw me. He said, "Dad, no phone. Put it down."

At that time, maybe I was making him uncomfortable or maybe I was irritating him. Then, I realized it was not appropriate behavior on my part. I thought how I would feel if someone did the same with me. It would feel like the other person is ignoring me.

I have heard lots of times from my friends or in public places how their teenagers make them frustrated and irritated with their devices. Nowadays you see lots of kids and teenagers always carrying some electronic gadgets.

The closer we are to something, the more limited the features we can actually see. When we are too close to a person, we can see only the limited traits of that person or kid.

For example, the other day, I met one of my friends. She was very excited and happy. Anyone could see just by looking at her that she was on top of the world. She said to me, "You know, I am so happy today. Do you know why?"

I asked her to please let me know what made her so happy.

She replied, "Finally, Daniel agreed to start playing soccer. You know, he took three months to say yes! I did so many things to make him agree. I made so many deals with him and now I am so excited!"

She had already bought sportswear for him: a New Jersey, short pants, and shoes. She showed me the photos. *I couldn't help but wonder whether she was celebrating her son's success or her own achievement.*

I know her and her son. Every couple of months, she talks about some issue with him. A few months ago, he didn't want to go out for swimming. Next, he was afraid to do martial arts. He was very excited about getting a rabbit and then, after two months, he had no clue where the rabbit was. He didn't care.

I am not complaining about what she does. My main point in this story is that this parenting is not really effective or fruitful. I think some parents unknowingly damage their children's self-esteem with the way they handle situations like this.

What is she teaching to her son while she is playing this role? I have a big concern over her attitude of being determined to get the results she wants no matter how many deals she has to make. Is that great parenting? What about the child's need for self-confidence, consistency, and commitment?

This boy may become very stubborn to get more out of her. Or, he may throw a big temper tantrum to get a more desirable outcome. Or, he may even play the victim or do something dramatic just to get more attention.

On another day, I was standing at a traffic light waiting to cross the road. There were a bunch of people on both sides and in front of me, a man was walking with a bag. A little girl, around 5 years old, was coming from the other side. Somehow, she hit the man's bag.

The man kept walking. He didn't bother her, but her mother started yelling at her very loudly, "WHY YOU DID THAT? YOU DON'T HAVE ANY COMMON SENSE!"

The little girl was in a playful mood. But now her mother nagged her in a public place. It will not only damage her self-confidence and self-respect, but also the trust in her mother.

Perception Makes a Difference ■

I heard a story about Mahatma Gandhi once. One day he was seated with some friends and leaders, reading public letters about what people thought about freedom. He was sharing those views with everyone present there.

In the process, he came across a letter which had three or four pages attached together with paper pins. He started reading it. It was full of negative views and abusive language. Other people got upset and said, "Throw it away."

Gandhi Ji just said, "Ok, but there is something good in here."

All the people were surprised.

He said, "All those pins which were used to attach these papers can be used again!"

How we perceive things in life makes a difference. We can help shape our children's perception and help them become positive by changing the way we put across our point to them. We can do this by choosing the correct/appropriate words and language in front of them, changing our internal chatter, keeping a watch on how we talk to others, and the words we use.

Words change thinking, and thinking changes our actions. Children start learning through observation. They build their non-verbal behavior and start using their behavior to build their non-verbal communication. Through listening, the child learns how to speak.

Just Do It, Or Let's Do It ■

"I am an action taker"

Most parents teach their kids either by rewarding for a good behavior or by punishment for a bad behavior. These two ways have been very popular for a long time to teach kids, but I believe these methods just modify their behavior, they do not exactly teach them. These methods have also been used a lot in psychology.

The reward and punishment principle has been used for classical conditioning by Pavlov and for instrumental condition by B.F. Skinner. Both used their methods to modify animal behavior and people began using these on their kids.

While they got results, there were also long-term consequences that were not always good. These methods need a big balance for them to work correctly, but usually, that balance doesn't happen.

Rather than using these methods we must use different methods. I recommend the **participation method**. What that means is we should focus on the cause of the behavior and not on the result. We need to figure out what is causing the problematic behavior because behind every behavior there is a reason. Then, we must ask the child about solutions.

The magic of this method lies in the tone of your voice and the questions you use. The questions must be open-ended and the tone of voice must be one that empowers and encourages the child. The key is to allow the child to explore and find the solution to their own problem.

For example, if you see your child hitting another child, stop and ask the child the reason for that action, without threatening. Find out what happened so you can be sure you fully understand the situation. Quite often, they were being antagonized by the other child and didn't know how else to get the other child to stop, so they took to hitting.

Once you know what happened, ask them questions about what else they could have done to solve the problem. When they present a solution, ask them to think about the consequences by reasoning as to what might happen if they chose that solution. Encourage them to come up with at least 3-4 ways to handle that situation better, the next time it comes up.

Now, instead of hurting the trust between the two of you by engaging in punishment, you have built trust with your child and given them an example of how to effectively solve the problem the next time if something like that happens and you aren't there to intervene.

The Mindset Matters ■
We need to focus more on psychology. The difference between life and death is often how resourceful we are. The resources available to us

amount only to 20% of our ability to adapt to a changing world. The rest 80% is psychological. That 80% determines the limits of what we are capable of achieving in life.

If you are psychologically strong, you can face the worst of the worst situations in life, no matter how bad the odds are, you can still survive. You can be happy in the worst situations if you are psychologically strong.

Here is something I noticed. Right now, I live in Australia, one of the best countries in the world. It is a developed nation and we have access to everything. four years ago, my wife and I went to Malaysia for a holiday. I watched some kids playing in the streets.

They were playing with a plastic bottle. They didn't have enough clothing to cover themselves, but they were having fun. I saw the same thing in my own country, India, as well. I had a neighbor whose kids were enjoying playing with things that weren't actually toys, just random things which they used to make their own games.

The tools are not really important, neither are the resources available to work with. What makes all the difference is the mindset. It isn't what's happening to you, it's what you're thinking and how you are feeling about that thing that makes all the difference. Through thinking comes feelings.

That's the thing I want to convey. Communication is powerful. Words are powerful. The power to communicate in the right way at the right time is most important. And the appropriate age for helping a child develop his/her communication skills is as early as possible. Start with your kids, even before they are born. Give them the right information. Talk to them while still in the womb. Let the child in there be attuned to the world outside.

I'm not saying you only need to tell them positive things. They need the right information, and that means helping them to learn to deal with the negative things in the world too. People die, accidents happen, people are killed, and robberies happen; you need to portray the complete picture of the things and events that happen in the outside world. You don't need to go into each and every detail from the very beginning, the thing is to help your child develop their own perception of what all happens, have his/her own views because perception determines the actions your child will take to handle the negative situations which they may encounter.

A Tragedy or an Opportunity

Let me share with you an example of the power of perception in determining how we respond to a situation. I learned this lesson from my father.

One day, we were sitting while my sister was doing something in the kitchen. She broke a glass. My mother immediately got upset, "You've destroyed the whole set!"

One glass was broken, and the set was not complete any longer unless we were to buy a replacement. My mother was thinking of the money she would have to spend to replace it. My father said, "It's just a glass, now we can buy a new set."

I was sitting right there, and thinking, "Look, they're my parents." I said, "Good! It's broken. I guess we can buy another one now."

That incident happened more than 20 years ago, and now my reaction resembles that of my father.

Two years ago, my wife was busy doing something while talking with me when she went to the bathroom and dropped her phone in the sink. For some reason, the sink had water in it. She started crying. I asked her, "What happened?"

When she explained what had happened, I told her it didn't matter. We could just buy another one. I'm very blessed and grateful to my father for teaching me that. Otherwise, I would have a tendency to get upset.

I noticed this in my relationship coaching as well. Because a small thing happens, and the two individuals have different perceptions of the situation, couples often start fighting. "You can't do this, you can't do that. How careless are you?" They start blaming each other because they were not trained in the right way to handle these situations.

If we teach our children to handle these negative situations in the right way, we are going to help bring more harmony and peace into their lives. When they grow up, they will do so with the right tools for happiness. Those tools can help and support them in their personal growth. The more personal growth they experience, the more peaceful and calm they will be as opposed to being frustrated, disappointed, and angry.

We need all our emotions, but not all of them help us grow. When something goes wrong, you may feel bad. That 'bad' feeling just means you need to fix something.

Chapter 2

❦ Understanding Where the Mindset Begins ❧

"Attracting Success feels easy and natural to me"

In day-to-day life, how we deal with people and how we see other people is on the basis of past experiences. What we see is based on our past experience.

Suppose I go outside this room and meet someone. I start judging them depending on my perspective of the person standing in front of me. If he does not talk to me, I may think, "Oh, that person is an introvert."

My past experiences are going to determine how I perceive this person. Those experiences play a very big role in our day-to-day life. How we perceive things and even what we perceive, according to Carl Jung, is determined by what we have inside our mind and body. We can both see the same thing out there in the world, but because everybody has their own unique experiences, we won't see it the same way.

Now, suppose that person starts talking to me. How am I going to talk? Subconsciously, my brain will tally his tone and expressions with my past experiences and I will respond in a way that best suits my own perception, on the basis of what I have done so far.

What kind of experience or learning we get out of the things that happen to us is determined on the basis of how we see those things. This is the power of the subconscious mind.

The Subconscious Mind

The subconscious mind is like a big memory bank. It has unlimited potential and virtually unlimited capacity. It is a permanent storage for all the memories that we accumulate in our daily lives. Nothing in there is erased or deleted. Whatever goes into the subconscious mind stays forever.

Now, although it holds the memories and the logical mind may know that these memories belong to the past, the subconscious mind doesn't. When something triggers a memory, the subconscious pulls it out of the storage and we experience it as if it were happening to us right then. That is why we react to those memories the same way we did earlier.

It begins developing even before we are born, and it plays a primary role in all our decision making. It leads us to react to the situations, circumstances, and people around us.

We accumulate memories and they are kept in a room, but most of us don't even have an awareness that such a room exists. Whatever we do in our day-to-day lives goes into that room and never leaves. It's like a storage vault. Whatever it is we are doing, whether it is learning or talking or listening, it doesn't matter. All of it goes into the mind and there is a particular room for it, although we may not be able to locate the particular place/location inside our brain where everything we encounter is stored.

Through our six senses that are working right now, we gather more than 60,000 bits of information every single second. The conscious mind can only handle between 5-9 chunks of that information at a time. Everything else goes into the subconscious mind.

Whatever we learn goes into the subconscious mind, and we forget about it. Once it is truly learned, we don't have to think about it. We just do it automatically. You can say it runs all the stuff that is in the background.

I was reading an article by Brian Tracy in which he writes that by the age of 21, you have already permanently stored more than 100 times the content of an entire encyclopedia. Encyclopedias are huge, but your brain is bigger.

In that context, the same thing applies. The abuse may have happened a long time ago, but it can still cause the person suffering at the age of 40. The memories aren't something we can erase, delete, or remove. That incident or event sticks in this subconscious mind.

The only thing about that event is - because it was a very intense we still remember it and it is still hurting us. Not consciously, but in the subconscious mind. The memory of that incident stays in the subconscious mind and continues to change our behavior. Consciously, we can reveal that.

If someone is suffering from some past event, that person won't suffer every single second or minute. S/he won't notice it unless something happens to trigger that memory. From where does that memory come? It comes from the subconscious mind. There is a big storehouse of memories somewhere in the brain. I don't know the exact location, but it's there.

The subconscious mind works in an autopilot mode. No one can control it. All bodily functions needed to survive, such as breathing, blinking, heartbeats, blood circulation, and things of that nature, are automatically controlled by the subconscious mind.

It also controls our hand gestures, facial expressions, and body postures. This is why you can use facial expressions to detect lies because lies are creative functions and so they go to the subconscious mind. You have to use your subconscious mind to be able to create a lie.

That's the thing the subconscious mind does. It controls things. No one can build the subconscious mind. It has that much power. It is a million times more powerful than the conscious mind. Whatever we do in our day-to-day lives, more than 90% of it is controlled by the subconscious.

On the basis of what we know now, the subconscious mind begins to develop in the womb itself. Lots of studies have been done which show that infants are able to remember things that happened to them while they were still in the womb.

The Conscious Mind

The conscious mind is your objective mind, the thinking portion of the brain. It has no memory and can only hold one thought at a time. The subconscious mind can hold lots of thoughts and memories, but the conscious mind can only hold one thought at a time.

The job of the conscious mind is to identify what is happening in your surroundings. Dr. Brian Tracy states that the conscious mind has four essential functions: identify incoming information, categorize it, analyze it, and compare it to the past experiences.

The information the conscious mind receives is any input coming from the senses such as sound, smell, taste, touch or feeling. The conscious mind is constantly observing and categorizing the things that are happening around us every moment.

As an example of how the conscious mind works, let's imagine that you are walking along the sidewalk and decide to cross the street. You step off the curb and at that moment, you hear the roar of an automobile engine. You immediately turn to look in the direction the sound waves are coming from. This is the first function: to identify what is happening.

The second function is 'comparison' or to compare. The brain compares the information about the car that we have seen and heard with all the previously stored information and experiences we have had with an automobile. The comparison is based on learning and memories in the subconscious mind. The second function uses the subconscious as well as the conscious mind.

It's like a Google search for some information with just one word 'mind'. Lots of things will show up about the mind. This is how the mind functions, particularly during sleep. Now what happens is, there is a lot of information available and the conscious mind starts digging for a particular information that we presently need.

The third function is to analyze. First, we identify, then we compare with previous experiences, and only then we begin to analyze. Why is this happening right now? What do I need to do about it? 'Analysis' is also a part of the fourth function: deciding.

Basically, the senses gather the information about the event happening in front of us and pass that information to the conscious mind. The conscious mind says, "Oh! That's what it is," and sends a signal to the subconscious mind to find all information about this in your database.

The subconscious mind pulls all the information it has stored about a similar event, the one which matches the sensory information about it and passes it to the conscious mind. The conscious mind then takes a decision as to what to do about it.

The conscious mind begins to develop after birth, at around 5 months of age, according to some recent studies conducted by cognitive neuroscientist Sid Kouider. This is the age when kids first start identifying what is going on around them, which is the first step towards developing the conscious mind. Scientists were able to compare the brain waves of infants to adults and noticed similar, although much slower, patterns in 5-month-old infants as were seen in adults.

Thinking and the Subconscious Mind ◼

The subconscious controls our thoughts because it commands which memories we see and how those memories are presented based on our previous experiences. The subconscious mind is like a magnet.

As I shared with you, the second role of the conscious mind is to compare. What happens is that if someone has a belief or a past experience, a bad one, with a particular person, the subconscious files away that particular guy's body structure. Maybe he's tall or strong and this person has had an experience where he comes to believe that such kind of people are bullies.

From then on, whenever that person sees somebody with a similar stature, the subconscious mind will bring up those memories and this will lead the person's conscious mind to believe that the two are same and conclude that this person is a bully too. That is how thoughts work.

At times, the logical mind can contradict the subconscious mind. In the earlier example, the logical mind may choose to reject the conclusion that this person is a bully. It may choose to say, "Not every time." This is how the conscious mind can help to rectify negative thinking.

Still, the subconscious is very powerful. It controls 90% of the thoughts we hold, and most of the time we are not even aware of those thoughts. I will share a personal experience with you. I used to do so many things unconsciously. I had a bad experience, and on the basis of that I would doubt other people, refuse to trust them. Consciously, I had no clue why I was doing that.

There was some incident in my subconscious mind that was controlling all my actions, my thinking, and my behavior, which was leading me to doubt other people, even my kids on whom I always kept checking. This is because the subconscious mind has that much power. It was influencing my conscious thinking as well.

Positive Affirmations

For positive affirmations to work, there are a few steps required. It isn't enough just to read something or say something. You have to read it with emotion and feel it.

I notice lots of people in their day-to-day-life use language in a negative sense. I don't often see people who want to lose weight say, "I want to lose weight." This is a very neutral statement, but they change it into a negative one, "I don't want to be fat."

The subconscious mind deletes negative words. Hence, it ignores the "don't" and just hears, "I want to be fat." Another way that would be positive for them to say could be, "I want to be healthy and fit."

"The subconscious mind cannot process negatives at all. If I tell you don't think of a Blue Car, what do you see?"

Positive affirmations must also be stated in a present tense like, "I am healthy and fit," because the subconscious mind cannot differentiate between real and unreal.

"The subconscious mind makes no difference between what's real and what's imagined."

Think what happens when we watch horror movies. Consciously, we know we are just watching a movie. We know the artists are not really getting hurt, they are just playing a role. The actress who was killed, we know we're going to see her again in another movie. Consciously, we know all of that. But what happens? When we start watching, we get scared. It does happen.

Similarly, say for fitness, we need to give information to the subconscious mind, "Right now, I am healthy and fit."

Most people don't put the emotion into it, and emotions play an important role in getting the subconscious mind to accept this information. When we just read something without any emotion, the subconscious mind will never accept it and take it inside the brain.

The first thing to do in order to make a change is that you have to believe you can. Many people refuse to even try positive affirmations. Without trying, without taking action, everything remains based on their personal past experiences and subconscious mind.

"Oh, no. That's not going to work."

If they haven't even tried it, how can they say it's not going to work? Affirmations work but done the right way. If you want to start your car but use your bike's key, it's not going to work. The same thing applies here. If you want to reprogram your subconscious mind, you have to believe it and then you have to pick the right key.

The proper way to have the right key is - first create a positive statement in the present tense. Second, bring your emotion into it. The emotions have more power than words. The words just impact 7% of the day-to-day life. What about the rest 93%?

These 93% of the emotions are in the body. We need to use those too and not just the 7%. That's the power. We need to use it, but people don't do that.

And to reprogram the brain, we have to repeat it again and again, and again. I'm 40 now. Something happened to me 25 years ago. That incident is still in my mind. It's not going to be replaced overnight. It needs time.

"My ability to conquer my challenges is limitless; my potential to succeed is infinite."

Making Changes Easier

To replace an old thought with a new one, we have to clean out the old one first. Actually, there's a catch here. Uninstalling old memories or old beliefs is a challenge. They aren't easy to remove.

I'll give you a small example. A long time ago, I was reading about how memory works. Memories are like wax. When the wax is warm and you put your hand in it, the wax imprints with everything that touches it.

When it cools down, you can see what was left behind, the fingerprints, the lines, and everything. However, once it cools down, you can add water to it and it won't melt away. Warm water will melt it a little bit, but that imprint will still be there. It takes very hot water to put the wax back in a state where the old imprint is gone and you can them make a new one there.

That's the power you have to use in order to get to your memories. That means you are going to be pretty uncomfortable initially. When you want to use positive affirmations, it's going to feel uncomfortable at first. It's very challenging, of course.

The subconscious mind has lots of power, and it isn't going to allow you to feel very comfortable. It will tell you to reject the affirmation. The conscious mind may know that this particular thought which you have been holding for the last 20 or 25 years is not helping you to grow, and you need to uninstall or replace this negative thought with a positive one. However, this is going to create a conflict between the subconscious mind and the conscious mind.

Being an intelligent being, you can use your conscious mind's power and resist the subconscious one. The subconscious mind doesn't really want to change, so any attempt to make a change is going to meet resistance. The subconscious mind is hard-wired for safety and stability. When you do something that changes what it considers to be safe and stable, it will fight you on it initially because it thinks you are putting yourself in danger.

This is known as the comfort zone. But the comfort zone is not really safe. The time of living in forests with lions and other predators is gone. There are still dangers, but we need to learn to meet our needs for safety and security in a resourceful, rather than an unresourceful way. The comfort zone is an unresourceful way of meeting those needs.

When, subconsciously, someone is fulfilling their needs in an unresourceful way, which is not sustainable and is hurting themselves or other people, that's a problem.

The subconscious mind works in this way. Imagine that it is a jar filled with, say, beer. You want to put something else into that jar, something healthier, like water. Now, you must first get rid of the beer so that you can have room for water in that jar.

The subconscious mind will resist your effort to get rid of the beer. It will remind you of how good it tastes, of the times when you've had fun drinking it, and all the reasons why you should keep that beer. It will bring those memories to mind. This is true about anything, even small habits.

However, your conscious mind has the final decision making power. You can consciously decide to pour out the beer anyway and choose to fill the jar with water.

For example, consciously, I decided that I wanted to wake up every morning at 4:30 am. That was a conscious decision. I didn't set any conscious decisions after that. I set three different alarms to make sure I would get up, but I slept through them.

Then, I decided that I wasn't going to set an alarm. Instead, I decided to use my subconscious mind and tell it, "I am going to wake up on time." Sure enough, I woke up. The subconscious mind is not always negative. It can be a very positive force in our lives.

Think of it this way. We have power through our subconscious mind. We should use that power because 90% is a lot of power. I changed my habit in just one day using that power. With the conscious decision that I wanted to wake up at that time without any alarm and then telling my subconscious mind what I wanted it to do, I was able to do it.

When you make a decision and employ your emotions to it, everything is possible. When we decide something emotionally, not logically, it is easier to do. When we bring the logic and the emotion together, it works even better.

I knew this guy who used to smoke at home. As soon as he found out that his wife was pregnant, he made a conscious decision to not smoke anymore. He quit without any struggle. He felt such powerful emotions about being a father that he didn't want to smoke around his wife and his baby. Those emotions came together with his logical, conscious decision making and he was able to make that change.

The conscious mind works logically a lot, sometimes even without emotions. I used to work with drug abusers and alcoholics as a clinical psychologist. In the rehabilitation industry, there are big frustrations especially because patients frequently relapse. People are treated and stay sober for 1-2 years, and then relapse.

The Subconscious Mind Isn't Logical

Why? I notice that when people come with their logical mind to get rid of this problem, they only stay sober for a limited time. Those people who come with emotional reasons stay sober for longer.

I also notice, the kids who come, especially teenagers between the ages of 16-19, don't use their emotions. They get rid of the drugs for just 3 or 4 months, and then relapse. The older people, especially those in their 30's who come with some emotional reasons are able to quit for longer periods. That is the power of emotions.

The subconscious mind works in these cases as well, especially with the drug abusers. I'll share a quick story about this. Drug abusers get a really good feeling after using some kind of substance. The subconscious mind says, "Oh, I'm feeling really good right now." That feeling goes into the subconscious and reinstates in the mind. In future, the subconscious mind has all that positive feeling and experience after taking the drugs. And this is why people relapse.

That experience, or whatever they got, comes from unresourceful behavior. Relapse happens because when they go outside the rehab facility, back to their communities, to their friends, and whenever they see, smell, hear or are reminded about the drugs, alcohol or cigarettes, their subconscious mind tells them, "Go have them, it's fun!"

It reminds them of all the positive experiences they have had while consuming those things. And anytime the person who is recovering encounters a struggle or a hardship, the subconscious mind reminds them of this.

For those who are struggling with making a change, to them I will say what I used to say to my patients, "You can't give up."

You may feel tempted, but you can stay away from that temptation as long as you make a conscious decision. Believe that you can change first. Believe, "Yes, I can change."

Chapter 3

⋘ Development of the Subconscious Mind ⋙

"My nature is Divine; I am a spiritual being."

All babies, whether human or animal, start learning before birth. I share this with you so that parents can focus more on raising a great generation, because this early learning is very important.

The Impact of the Initial Years

They cultivate 85 percent of their intellect, personality, and skills by age five. - Brain Development and Early Learning, Wisconsin Council on Children and Families

"The human brain develops more rapidly between birth and age five than during any other subsequent period"
- Brain Development and Early Learning,
Wisconsin Council on Children and Families

As you know, between the ages of 6 to 8 years, a child's learning potential is at its maximum. Before this age, a person lays the foundation of his or her subconscious mind and the rest of their lives will keep adding and learning, changing old learnings, and deleting some old files. Some will become distorted over time as well. This process carries on continuously and is still going on within you and me, right now. Whatever we learn, if we repeat it again and again, it is going to be very firm.

Here are some examples. A young child starts learning how to ride a bike. In the beginning, he may fall and get hurt, but after some time he learns it and never has to learn it again. He can ride after 20, 30, 40, or even 50 years later. Moreover, he can talk and look around without thinking about it or paying any attention to it because it is imprinted in his subconscious mind. This is called subconscious learning. You can see the same principle in different areas of your life, like while cleaning your teeth, driving, or talking on the phone, as well as in many other activities.

Babies Before Birth

Learning begins even before birth. Yesterday, I was reading an article written by a doctor who is a hypnotherapist and has done a lot of research on this subject. He discovered, through his hypnosis patients, that babies begin learning even before they are born, while they are still in the womb.

At the time the baby's brain starts working, it begins to pick up the mother's emotions. These become the first memories in the subconscious.

Dr. David Chamberlain, the author of Babies Remember Birth, mentioned that it doesn't matter if the baby is one week or two weeks old in the womb, they can feel what's going on in the outside world. They start feeling the things that are happening. And they learn emotions from their mother. Her emotions teach them how to react in a particular situation.

There's a case study of this guy, a 6-year-old boy. He is very good and normal, but he has some issues at school. The school says he doesn't want to do his homework and assignments. He's capable of doing these, but he doesn't want to do it.

These parents went to see a doctor. They said to the doctor, "Please help us."

He played this game with the child. It was like hide and seek, and all of a sudden the boy was like, "Okay. Ready or not, I am coming."

The hypnotherapist picked up the signals. Then he started talking to the parents. "Tell me about the time when you guys conceived him."

The lady, she was a little ashamed and admitted that when she found out she was pregnant, she was not really happy. She was upset for some time.

But the six-year-old, who was sitting next to his mom said, "No, she was not upset. She was mad."

The doctor looked at her.

She said, "He's right. I was mad. And my husband was upset too."

They never told this to him. After he was born, they started loving him and all, but before that, they had a different view. Both husband and wife didn't want him to come to the world. The boy experienced this. They were very upset and really didn't want him.

Another lady, an adult, shared a similar experience. Her story came out through hypnotherapy. But with the boy, there was no need to hypnotize him, he remembered what happened when he was in his mother's womb.

This is a thing which happens. And the same is the case with music. Whatever experience the lady has, is the same experience the baby will have. If the lady is really brave and strong, the baby will develop brave and strong feelings as well. Sometimes that may not happen though, but there's a different reason there.

As per my review, these things happen. Kids who have never undergone any kind of artistic training, still are really good in that. Why? Because the power of the subconscious mind is there. They've been through it, like maybe before birth or something, they did their imaginary thinking, watching something.

They build their power there. The subconscious mind is working for them, not against them. And when they grow up, because they didn't have any kind of conflict between the conscious and the subconscious mind, the subconscious mind works in a positive way.

Some studies have shown that when a woman is pregnant and sings to her baby, the baby can hear her more clearly than if she is just speaking. That experience is the beginning of the development of subconscious mind.

Before birth, the brain is more active and uses more energy than any other area of the body. 97% of the energy a child takes in while in the womb goes to the development of the brain. All the senses develop at this time. Language begins to develop at this time. Neurons too develop at this time. This is also when the baby begins to learn communication.

"Sensory and brain mechanisms for hearing are developed at 30 weeks of gestational age, and the new study shows that unborn babies are listening to their mothers talk during the last 10 weeks of pregnancy and, at birth, can demonstrate what they've heard."

– Pacific Lutheran University

It is also when the earliest memories begin to form. These early memories are attached to the neurons that have developed and consist of the emotions that were felt by the infant at that time. Those memories will become stronger as the child later explores the world.

Fetal origins is a scientific discipline that emerged just about two decades ago, and it's based on the theory that our health and well-being throughout our lives is crucially affected by the nine months we spend in the womb.
– Annie Murphy Paul, author of Origins

Early Communication Experiences

Communication is not just verbal, it's non-verbal as well. And this communication happens in several different ways. We send messages to one another, share our feelings and emotions, our behavior and our words. We communicate through movies and theater, cell phones, online conference calls, instant messaging, etc.

Through communication, I can sense the person's emotions. Our senses are a form of communication, too. Words are one form of communication, non-verbal is another, and our senses are a third. The tone of the voice that is used tells us everything about what is going on within the other person. The tone of the voice used and what our senses detect about the other person are very important parts of communication.

Sharing our knowledge, experiences, and feelings in this way allows us to feel connected to one another, and those connections begin before birth, while we are still in the womb. When a woman is pregnant, she begins talking with her baby.

Some of this communication is not spoken. For example, a mother might feel her child bump against her belly. She caresses and taps the spot where she feels the child in her. The child moves in response to her action and kicks back. This game can go on for quite some time. The more she "speaks" to her baby, whether verbally or non-verbally, the stronger the connection between them grows.

When my wife was pregnant, my unborn baby would kick her. When I touched the spot where he had kicked, he would kick again. He would hear my voice and respond to my touch. It was no accident, as this repeated many times during the pregnancy. It was clear that my child was doing this intentionally as a form of communication.

When babies are in the womb, they can listen, they can hear, and they can respond accordingly. It is during this time in the womb that the subconscious mind begins to develop as well.

One of the religious texts I read, the Mahabharata, talks about this. The warrior, Abhimanyu, mentioned in those scriptures is said to have learned all of his war strategies by listening to his Uncle (Lord Krishna) talk to his mother about them while he was still in the womb. When he grew up, he was able to use those strategies in battle.

Connection and Communication ■

Once the baby is born, everyone else begins to communicate with him/her. This communication also happens in different ways. Sometimes people speak using sensible language, and sometimes nonsensical language. The goal is still the same: to form a connection with the baby.

Science has proven that the way a baby suckles when its mother is feeding is its own unique form of communication. Babies suckle faster when they are bored, and slower when something has captured their attention. How they suckle is their own language.

The communication forms a connection, a bonding, between two human beings. This bonding is a must, not only between the baby and the parents but also between the baby and other human beings. We have a built-in need to communicate and connect with one another.

"Today, I am brimming with energy and overflowing with joy."

Communication Outside the Womb ■

Babies understand language straight away when they are born. I will use my son's example here. He was born in Australia, an English speaking country. All of his teachers and friends in his childcare center spoke English. However, my son was able to understand Hindi.

I noticed, one day when my wife was watching one of her comedy soap operas, which was in Hindi, as soon as my son heard the program, his head turned to look for it. He recognized it although we had never played that program around him. I wondered how it was he knew it.

After talking with my wife, I discovered the reason. While she was pregnant, she used to watch this program daily. He had learned to recognize it in the womb!

That is the power of learning which takes place even before birth and the memories that develop at that time. He was exposed to this program before birth, and now he knew it. Science has proven, my son is not an isolated incident. Babies are able to distinguish between their mother's native and foreign languages immediately after birth.

A child who is conceived in a foreign country actually has an advantage over one who migrates to a foreign country later. A child who learns one language in the womb and is then exposed to another one shortly after birth develops more neurons and at a faster rate as the brain tries to assimilate this new information. From the age of 0 to 3, the brain develops faster and there is more neuron growth than at any other time in life.

A child's brain is affected by any new stimulus. Something stimulates the child, the neurons develop more quickly. Imagine that the child's brain is like a field. When a farmer wants to grow something new in the field, he plants seeds. He then waters and fertilizes those seeds so that they begin to grow. After a few weeks, some of those seeds will die, but the stronger ones will grow even stronger. This same thing happens in the brain.

The child's brain, at that time, is fertilizing the seeds of language that are being planted in it. It's growing very fast. The more the child's brain is stimulated, the more neurons are created, and more neurons mean more experiences. Exposure to new situations facilitates to stimulate brain growth and helps the child later in life.

Children can learn more than 8 languages before the age of 6. The earlier they learn, the easier those languages are to learn. This is because their brains are still growing and their neurons are developing at an incredibly fast pace. This is what makes learning so easy for a child.

For an adult, we may struggle to learn even basic life skills like driving a car. This is because the brain becomes like a fixed structure once we become an adult.

By the age of 3, the maximum number of neurons have been generated. Different stimulations and situations produce that neuron growth. Which language we use with our children, whether English, Hindi, Punjabi, German, Spanish or Farsi does not matter. What matters is that we speak to them and how we do that. Communication has an impact.

"I am the architect of my life; I build its foundation and choose its contents."

Communication Builds Memories

The neurons that are created when a child hears language being spoken to them have the power to retain emotions and build memories. What are memories? We can't see memories inside the brain but still, we can recall everything. Memories are experiences that have been attached to the neurons. Feelings are memories.

Kids have memories. And how do we teach kids? With language.

If you are a parent, you may have noticed that your child is still complaining to you about things you did to or didn't do for them when they were little. For example, a teenager may bring up things you did when they were in 5th grade or even younger. Sometimes they do it out of fun.

You may have wondered how this could happen. Exterior things always remain in our minds. Always. Whether it was a good thing that happened or a bad one, it's always recorded in our brains. Our little ones have the power to retain those past feelings. On the basis of those memories, the child builds a perception of the world around them.

This is why the exact same situation can trigger a different reaction in different people. If I ask a person what s/he thinks about bungee jumping, for instance, and how s/he feels about it, I will get very different responses from various individuals. One person might hold their hands up, laugh, shake his/her head vehemently, and say, "Not me. No. Not ever."

Ask that same person's spouse or partner and you might hear, "Oh! I would love to!"

As you can see, the exact same event, two different people, they perceive it in different ways. This is because of our interpretation of what that event or situation means to us. The interpretation comes about because you have some kind of memory related to it. Either it could be a personal experience or one that you may have observed.

Perception: Mother of Miscommunication

Miscommunication happens because of the personal experiences and memories of the individuals in a conversation. Those personal experiences and memories distort the message we receive, and this causes the misunderstanding. We fail to interpret correctly what the other person is trying to say.

This distortion is totally different from a lack of communication. If I communicate something to you in my native language, Hindi, you might not understand the words, but you can understand the expressions. The tone I use will tell you whether I am really excited or upset or frustrated or depressed. I can still communicate my feelings to you even if the exact meaning of my words is not getting through to you.

Those memories can form in the beginning, within the first thousand days of life. These first thousand days of life are very important for children as they are the foundation for life. This foundation needs to be very strong.

How we lay the foundation is very important, not just physically, but mentally as well. People often worry about the child's physical well-being, what they eat, when they sleep, and all that stuff. And that's good. But what about the brain? What about the emotions? What about the psychology? So, let's talk about what people, especially the parents, can do to lay a strong foundation that addresses both the mind and the body.

How we talk to them can make a big difference. I have seen people, and maybe you've noticed this as well, from dysfunctional families. Being raised in a dysfunctional family impacts children a lot. Another kid, born in another family, after growing up, even if they go through the same things, are going to have a different experience. They build their beliefs there, and on what basis? Their personal experience.

Their experiences and their feelings are what they learn. They learn through observation and what has been taught to them on the basis of that. So, the first thousand days are really very important. For me, I like to say the first 7-8 years of life, but especially the first thousand days because those are the days when there is maximum learning potential.

My main focus in writing this chapter is to emphasize the importance of how to communicate with our kids. We need to communicate with them in the right way so that they can grow well and further develop their lives.

The Power of Early Childhood Experiences

A few months ago, I met a lady who was 32 years old. She'd been in a couple of relationships but was never able to establish a long-term relationship. When I interviewed her, it finally came out that when she was 5 years old, she was abused and, at that time, she developed a belief, "Men are despicable!"

That event created memories for her, and because of that incident, she suffered for the next 27 years - all because of one incident. That bad memory, that one event, began dictating all her decisions surrounding relationships with men. And she didn't even know it.

This is an example of how powerful these memories can be. One event is enough to change anyone's life. I focus on how powerful these early childhood experiences are in determining the future of our kids because they are going to be the future of our nation and our world. If we take care of them physically, but not so much mentally and psychologically, we are crippling their ability to grow into healthy adults.

Experience Is the Real Legacy

Experience has a lot of power. Before birth and up to the age of 3, the whole period of about 4 years is time exclusively for exploration. Let them explore. As much as they explore, they are going to learn more leading to the creation of more neurons which further leads to more memories. That's the main thing.

Once they know how to continue nourishing their curiosity level, they are going to experience success in their lives. When parents start saying to their children, "Don't do this. Don't do that. Don't. Don't. Don't," what is going to happen in that environment? The child becomes afraid of doing anything. They become afraid of everything. The child develops what is known as learned helplessness. S/he becomes afraid of doing anything and loses his/her initiative.

Studies have been done by Dr. Martin Seligman, the father of positive psychology, on how people develop this learned helplessness. In one of his studies, he put dogs in harnesses. The dogs were given electric shocks at random intervals. They had no way to avoid the shocks.

Then he put them in separate cages. One side of the cage was electrified, the other side was not, and a short dividing wall was put between the two sides. If the dog wanted to go out, all it had to do was jump out.

What happened? The dogs did not even try. They had learned helplessness. They didn't believe there was a point to their efforts.

When we keep telling children, "Don't. Don't. Don't," the brain starts narrowing. The brain stops exploring.

Seligman then conducted another set of experiments, looking for a way to prevent learned helplessness from setting in altogether. This time he started by placing the dogs in boxes/cages and let them discover that they could escape without any shocks, at first. Then, he would put them into the harnesses where they couldn't escape the shocks for some time.

When he put them back in the boxes/cages, these dogs never gave up. As soon as they had the ability to do it, they avoided the shocks and jumped out.

The same thing happens to us as well. We can explore something and this is good, but when the door is closed and all we hear is "Don't. Don't. Don't," we learn helplessness, instead. When that child grows into an adult with that much helplessness and something comes up, s/he is not ready to take the steps to address that.

Learned helplessness creates a comfort zone for people, and they are too afraid to take a step outside of their comfort zone because of that helplessness. This learned helplessness happens at a very early age.

Abuse and the Subconscious Mind

A bruise should not be the requirement for evidence of parental abuse. There are many other ways a child can be harmed. While this list may not be all-inclusive, it is meant to expand on the traditional definition of child abuse. Most Nations recognize some aspects of sexual abuse, physical abuse or neglect, but fail to fully address them.

Most of them completely disregard mental, verbal, emotional, financial, and spiritual abuse. This list provides an opportunity to explore, evaluate, and discuss other types of child abuse. Abuse of any kind can ruin a child's future, instilling emotions and thoughts of fear, mistrust, and unworthiness.

Chapter 4

◄ Parenting Is Tough ►

'Happiness is a choice. I base my happiness on my own accomplishments
and the blessings I've been given.'

Parenting is one of the longest projects of life for the parents. Before I go into the subject of abuse, I just want to say that parenting is tough. I would want to meet any parents who have a plan to make their kids one of the worst children of the earth or universe. So far, I haven't seen any parents who have such a desire or wish. All the parents I meet want their kids or children to become nice people and good citizens.

I hear them tell me the things they want for their children:

Self-love and self-trust, compassion for all, being a good human and doing well at school and then in life, respect for themselves and others.

All these characteristics are what parents want for their children. The problem is their perception, or what they think, about how they want their children to get those things. When your perception is involved, you start judging people on the basis of your knowledge. You start judging your kids. If they have all these traits, then they are good human beings, a good son or daughter. If not, they are bad.

The real question is, how are you going to instill these good qualities in your kids? It's not like you can install some software or download an app. Science has proven that your child starts learning when they are in the womb. You might ask how they can learn when they can't see.

Science says they learn through listening and through shared emotional experiences with the mother. Whatever the mom feels, the baby feels too, and these feelings create the first memories. Later, when hearing develops, they add the sounds they hear to their memories. While there is no logical or cognitive learning, there is plenty of learning in the subconscious mind.

Raise your child totally judgment free. Don't try to fulfill your desires or your wishes through your child.

People want to eat free range eggs, chicken, and organic fruits and vegetables. They know this lifestyle produces healthier chickens and plants, which means their food will be healthier too. But they do not allow their kids to grow free range. They create a set of rules and regulations to control their kids and restrict their kid's curiosity and playfulness.

Creativity comes through curiosity, but instead, they check and control their kid's behavior all the time.

Why? If you know the behavior isn't harmful to the child, don't stop them. Give them the right direction instead of saying 'no'.

Overconcern Limits a Child's Growth

"My life is just beginning."

The social environment where we live has different expectations for kids, not only from parents but also from the society. Parents have different parameters for their kids and the world has different perceptions. These expectations and perceptions limit children's capacity to dream.

Much of these expectations come out in questions such as - what is your son or daughter doing, what is their major subject, and how much he or she scored this year.

Supporting Your Child

When I was 14 years old, I used to whistle. At that time and in the neighborhood where I was living, people did not see this as a decent habit. One of our neighbors complained to my father that I was whistling. He told my father, "It's not good, especially for those who belong to good families. This activity is suited to goons."

My father was a very calm and straight-forward man. His reply amused me. He said, "I don't find anything wrong with whistling. In fact, I do the same whenever I feel happy and excited."

After that, the neighbor never complained again. The reason was my father's reply to him.

I know people who tell me that their old man or mother always listened to the complainer rather than to them and, without asking them anything, they were punished a lot. They never forget those days. This leads to kids losing their trust in their parents.

Allowing Mistakes

Overconcerned parents prevent their kids from making mistakes. Successful people and successful inventors totally agree that more successful people make more mistakes than anybody else. Allow your kids to make mistakes, as long as it's not a threat to their lives.

Some parents go so far as to make decisions on behalf of their children even after they are grown up! A child can understand his strength and weakness better than anybody.

When I was just 11 years old, my parents asked me if I wanted to go to a boarding school. My answer was a big 'YES'.

They arranged everything for me. Boarding school was very far from my parents' residence, almost 3500 Km. It took two days and one night traveling by train in the 1980's. I was very excited to go. My mother was emotional. I saw tears in her eyes and her voice was full of emotions as she bid me goodbye.

At the boarding school, a few things happened. The first being, it was an emotional roller coaster ride. I was away from my parents for the first time. And this is where I was abused.

The Unexpected Experiences

"I forgive those who have harmed me in my past and peacefully detach from them."

I had just turned 11 when I went to the boarding school. I was very excited about going there and about being away from my parents. My mother was crying. She couldn't imagine me being away. I was confident. I was a big boy.

I reached the boarding school and started missing my family. Literally, for the next two months, I cried every evening. Apart from that, initially, there was no problem at all. I was being fed and looked after very well.

There was a little bit of ragging by the senior boys. They used to come in and do some funny stuff and made fun of us new ones there. They would tell us to go and shine their shoes or do their laundry or wash their dishes. This was part of it, as well. If they made a mess, they would tell us to clean it up. They would also punish those of us who didn't do as ordered.

At first, when I got there, I felt alone. It was hard for me to get comfortable in my new surroundings. I'd never been in this kind of a situation before.

Life had always been relaxed and I'd been able to have fun. Here, there was pressure. Every morning I had to wake up at 5:00 am. Every night I had to go to bed at 9 o'clock. I had to study and the principal was very unkind.

He used to come into our room to check on us. If someone was found sleeping when he was supposed to be studying, the principal used to bash him very badly with a stick. I became afraid.

There were ten of us who were sixth-grade students. All of us were in one room. It was a very big dorm room. One of the guys was taller, stronger, and older than I was. I think he was 13 or something. One day, he came to me. I was pretty innocent at the time.

This boy knew all about the sexual things. I had just heard about this stuff but had no experience and no thought about it yet. He came over to me and held me. I didn't think much about it. He offered me some of his old things like games and toys, as incentives, which were a lot better than other students. He kissed me on my cheek.

I thought then, "No. This is not good," but I was not able to complain about him to anybody. There was no one I could go to, to talk about what happened to me out there. This happened to me three or four times. It wasn't sexual, exactly, but the way he was treating me made me feel uncomfortable.

He was a little older than me and I felt, after that, that something was not good. Somehow, we stopped talking and seeing each other. That was it. That was all that happened.

And then another guy, about my age, lived in the same room. We used to sit together and sometimes we would sleep together . Another guy in our dorm saw us together and made a story out of it. He told everyone we were doing things that were wrong.

There was no sexual involvement between us, nothing like that. It was a matter that this kid missed his family and I missed mine and we were in the same boat, emotionally. We were seen sitting together and talking, and that guy made this story. People in the school started talking about us. People started making more stories and the seniors started making fun of us. Those experiences impacted me a lot.

My self-confidence became low. Before I went to boarding school, I was very confident. My father was always proud of me. Always. I was the one who never hesitated to do anything. I was an action taker.

When I had been 9 or 10 years old, I used to go with my father for runs every morning. I was somewhat naughty as well. If someone tried to fight with me, I was always willing to go. What came later, I'll discuss in the following chapter.

"I learn from every situation I encounter."

The Consequences of the Experiences

After that incident, my confidence was gone. I stopped speaking much. I stopped doing anything. I would eventually regain it, but it took me a long time. That incident changed everything.

I mentioned this because I had no support there. I was away from my parents, and there was no counselor or psychologist. There was no one in the whole school to help me adjust. There was no facility that was sensitive to what kids were going through. Nobody talked to us to ask us what was happening or what was going on or if we had any problems or issues. Nothing like that.

One day, I was very sick in the boarding school. There was no one there to look after me. I was in the dining hall. One of the guys, a senior from grade 11, saw that I wasn't eating my food. He was a very nice guy and asked me what happened. I don't remember his name, but I still remember his face.

I told him I didn't feel good. He consulted a doctor and said that I needed to eat some light food. He was the first guy I saw who supported me. Before that, no one supported me. That guy really stood by me and raised the issue to the administrators of the boarding school.

My going to the boarding school was not a mistake. I chose to go there, but I didn't know what was going to happen to me when I got there. I can't say my choice was wrong. It was right, but the incidents which happened were not.

The Benefits of Experience

The purpose of allowing a child to make mistakes is to help them gain experience. The experiences I had were traumatic. If I knew, before I went, that such things could happen, maybe I could have taken more precautions. I had no idea what would happen and no one was there to tell me.

Nowadays, a lot is done beforehand to prepare the students. They have orientations and there are awareness classes. Last year, my brother-in-law, who is 18 years old, joined a university. He would be boarding and this was his first such experience.

I shared with him everything I'd gone through. I told him about all of my experiences, the things that could happen there, and how he could look after himself. I would call him twice a month to give him support while he was there. I didn't talk to him as a brother-in-law. I talked to him as a friend.

Sometimes his parents won't allow him to do something and I would let him do it on my responsibility. But before I did, I gave him the full scenario of the worst situation and the consequences it could lead to. I would ask him the questions of what could happen and how he could handle it if it went wrong. I prepared him gave him a full orientation beforehand.

As a small example, three months ago, he went to a kind of a fashion show because he wanted to become a model. He asked his parents, and they refused to let him do it. They told him they didn't believe that he should go there. So he called and asked me what he should do.

I told him I would talk to his parents and get them to allow him to go, but before that, I wanted to know a few things. I asked him why he was going there, what he was going to do when he got there, what the reason was that it mattered to him so much, what was the worst that could happen, and how he would handle it if it did.

He won my confidence because he had a pretty good awareness of the worst thing that could happen there and how and what to do about it if it did. So I gave him my permission to go.

Raising Awareness of the Dangers

Awareness is the first thing a parent should provide when a child wants to explore something a parent doesn't think is a good idea. Mentally prepare them for what might happen and help them think through solutions to the potential problems that could come up.

For example, if something happens financially, mentally prepare the child for what to do in that case. In this way, we can help them avoid suffering emotionally. Physically, what can happen? If we can get them to think about this, we can help them avoid such situations.

Obviously, this technique needs to wait until they are old enough to understand. Till then, we can do it for them. If they are just 2-3 years old, they can't understand it. But once they are older, they can.

"At the end of the day, the most overwhelming key to a child's success is the positive involvement of parents."
Jane D. Hull

Helping Infants and Toddlers Explore and Adapt ■

My son just turned three. He doesn't like going to childcare. They just promoted him to a bigger room. It makes things really challenging for me, sometimes. I don't always know how to handle this little guy.

I am learning every day. Yesterday, I spoke to the director. I don't know if I'm just overly fussy or emotional or what, but I find myself concerned about the way they speak to my son. I am very concerned about communication.

This morning, while writing, I was thinking to myself, "He is three. He has just started deriving meaning from the things that are happening to him. He doesn't understand it, but still, he's going to make meaning out of these."

He is going to begin forming beliefs based on this, and actually, that is my main concern. I spoke to the daycare lady and she got a little rough with me and said, "You need to understand this."

I told her, "I do understand. I understand the problem, but my main concern is about him. I'm his father. I'm also a thinker and a psychologist. It is my job to think about this."

And it isn't just my training that gives me a cause for concern. I have some experience with this as well. Abuse is not just of one kind. Because of all the things that happened to me, I am always careful now.

I've been through these situations; I've had these experiences, and they changed me. Those experiences, I know, were not good. Everybody undergoes certain experiences in life which may not be that pleasant and can deal with those in one of the two ways. Sometimes they come out aggressive or negative. I've never become aggressive or violent against things, but I know what it can do. These experiences can change anybody's life.

My son is not able to understand how to adapt to his new situation at the childcare. He is having trouble adjusting. In that situation, we can give the child an orientation. He could be taken to the other room, which is smaller and where there are lesser kids. Or, rather than just moving him to a new room, they could start three or four weeks earlier by sending him into the room where he would be spending most of his time, let him go for 2-3 hours and learn a few things with the other kids, so that he can see what will happen and how things are. He could be made to get accustomed to the surroundings slowly without much force.

The same thing can be applied to any other kids too. When we decide to allow them to go out and do something, we must be careful what we're allowing them to do and how it will affect them mentally. When they are old enough to understand, we can talk and explain. When they are too young for talking or understanding, we need to be involved and give them experiences by being with them. If you can't be involved or watch over their activities, have someone else available to be with them.

In my son's new room at the daycare, there is a little girl too who is 4 or 5 years old. She doesn't know much. She pointed to this other boy and said, "Hey, there is a bad boy." She is labeling that boy as a bad boy. What is going to happen? That boy is going to start thinking to himself, "I am a bad boy," because he doesn't know better.

In that situation, the parent or the educator must be involved there to watch over any false pretensions being spread amongst the kids. They are too small and yet to learn a lot. They have a very limited vocabulary to explain what they want to say. The parents or educators must watch the language being used by the children in regards to other children and think about how it is going to impact them. These children are at an age where they are making meaning out of everything with very limited terms they know how to use.

We can't stop them. Without exploring, they can't do anything. They need to get experiences and learn things. Experience is the only thing which will never go away. Whatever experiences they have, whether bad or good, stay in the mind. We use those experiences, sometimes subconsciously, to make up our minds and make decisions. So, we need to let them explore and experience things, but with involvement.

We can't stop them from making mistakes. We need to let them make those mistakes, but we need to be there to help them learn from those things. Making a mistake is really good to learn and to let them know to be happy even if things go wrong and that it's okay to make mistakes as well.

My body is healthy; my mind is brilliant; my soul is tranquil.

The Impact of Language ■

I was at the Royal Melbourne Zoo with my wife. It was a really very beautiful place. As I passed all the security procedures, I saw a beautiful family. It was a couple and their two sweet girls. One was around 4 years old and the other around 7. I felt very good seeing them at that time.

They were about 70 to 80 meters away from us, so I could see them but not hear their conversations. As we got closer, I noticed that the elder girl was asking something from her father. The guy's reaction was very weird.

He broke my imagination of that family. He shouted at that little one so loudly, "WHAT'S WRONG WITH YOU?"

The words are still echoing in my mind, and I can still hear the way he said it to her. I can't forget it. As soon as I heard these words, I felt a lot of pain in my heart and I still feel it while I write about this incident. I wonder about that little angel.

That one incident could change her whole life. How she goes on to handle the impact of this on her little heart and mind, how she faces this pain, and what meaning she takes from this sentence will make a big difference in her future. There are lots of emotions related to this incident: anger, pain, and frustration.

I worry because it is at this stage we start building our beliefs. Emotional experiences are the building blocks of belief because they are the basis of our memories.

Think about this: if someone that angry, loud, and furious, were telling you or your child, "What's wrong with you?" what meaning would you give it? What would your reaction be? How would you handle it?

Most people would take it to mean that there is something wrong with them. They would begin to think things like, "I am not good enough," or "I am defective."

If you find more meanings to it, that's great. Please share them with me too. I hope you can see what I am trying to say and that we are on the same page here.

Lots of mental issues are being seen in this present era because of the way we are living now and thinking about the future. What we are doing is pinching or stealing freedom from our kids.

Think of it this way: If we plant the seeds of Babool, then we will get Babools. If we plant seeds of mangos, we will get mangos. In this instance, the seeds we are planting is the language we are using, and this is determining the future for ourselves and our kids. What a frightful harvest we are getting because we are careless with the seeds we are planting!

If we keep doing such things, what will happen? We will continue getting the same results with no change. This is pure insanity, a kind of vicious cycle that we need to break.

A long time ago, when I had just started my professional journey and was enjoying each and every moment, Dr. Shahi Prateek, my project-in-charge called me. She said, "I want you to do some public speaking."

As soon as I heard this, guess what I did? Do you think I was jumping around, my face delighted, smiling, very happy, and feeling relaxed? Nothing like that. I was kind of shocked. My face got white and my breath stopped for a moment. My palms became sweaty and my heart was palpitating. My body's energy almost completely drained and my thought process stopped for a while.

I asked her, "Is it possible for someone else to do it?"

She replied strongly, "No."

Then, she reassured me, "I know you can do it. I know you have all the skills and guts required to do this. You know your content. You can do it easily."

After that meeting, I decided I would do it. There were only four days before I was to give my first presentation. During those days, I practiced only one thing - my own internal chatter. I replaced all my "can't" thoughts with "I can do this."

I kept saying, "I can do it. I can do it." Gradually, I started using other words, which helped me to get rid of my fear. I said these sentences with all my emotions, I really meant those words in my feelings and gestures, while creating a picture in mind of exactly how I wanted to see myself. I imagined giving a talk that I would enjoy listening to and behaving in a way which I was supposed to on the stage.

I used all my sensory channels to prepare for that day. What this does is to fire up the neuro-brain and create a desirable image. I kept practicing my language and this helped me to create a new image of myself. After some time, it became a part of my subconscious mind.

Our subconscious mind starts building before our birth. Science has proven that a child can hear while he is in his mother's tummy and he can feel the emotions she expresses as well. There are even a few cases that have been reported of kids remembering trauma they experienced while they were in their mother's tummy.

Now, just imagine, if a baby can feel and express emotions during that time, it means that babies are building their subconscious mind. The main or key role is played by the words that we use to communicate with each other or with our child.

Human beings are meaning-making machines. We create and assign meaning to each and everything based on our experiences and beliefs. When words are spoken, we look for the meaning of those.

The tools we use to assign meaning when we are first learning are the tone of voice, facial expressions, body language, and the context in which a word is spoken. This first experience with that word goes into our subconscious mind and becomes part of our subconscious communication.

Through subconscious communication, we build our ego, which is, to say, our belief about who we are and what we are capable of doing. Reactions come from the subconscious mind. They are sudden, spontaneous responses to the stimulus in our environment.

The subconscious mind has its own system of how it works. Our conscious mind has the capacity to process between 5 to 9 chunks of data at a time. Dr. Mehiney from The Flow states that our brain receives more than 200.000 kilobits of information every second. It processes only about 150 bits or about 7 chunks. Where does the rest of the information go? Straight to the subconscious mind.

Ego has two faces. The first can help us. It's the positive things we believe to be true about ourselves. The other goes against us. It's all the negative things we believe to be true about ourselves.

The ego is like an empty container. It's all up to us what we would like to store in it. It doesn't matter how we store it, what matters is what we store in it. It doesn't matter if the spoon you are using to eat something is of silver or gold. If what you have in it is honey, it's going to taste sweet and if what you have in it is a bitter medicine, it's going to taste bitter.

Communication is the only way human beings can connect with others. Our communication is either verbal or non-verbal. Verbal communication is through language or words. The words we use create 7% of the impact we have on others. The rest of the communication is non-verbal and includes things like the tone and pitch of our voices while we speak.

37% of the impact we have on others comes from the tone and pitch of our voice. It makes a big difference. The other 56% comes from the gestures, facial expressions, and the body language we use.

Recognition

I was speaking with a coaching friend of mine who shared with me a very amazing experience that happened to her. One of her friends was appreciating her daughter, Dee. My coaching friend's friend was complimenting her on how gorgeous her daughter was and how pretty and so on. When my friend expressed her appreciation for that woman's daughter, she not only ignored it but neglected the compliment.

I can't help but wonder what that lady just taught her daughter. That little girl could take this as she was not worthy of appreciation. One of my doctor friends asked me, "Why would someone not like being complimented?"

I gave my thoughts on this and came up with a few ideas about human behavior. First, that person has some doubt about it. Second, there may be a lack of self-love. All these come when someone does not get the right environment and develops a belief or fear that they are not good enough.

The 4R Model of Teaching

Reliance. Rebellion. Results. Realization.

The 4R model of instruction is not just a model for children, but also an adult model of growth. This model works in any environment where someone is trying to develop or grow whether on a personal level, a professional level, business level or a relationship level.

Reliance

During this stage of instruction, the student is reliant on the instructor for everything. Think of an infant. They rely on others for everything when they are born. They rely on their parents for feeding, for changing nappies, for a shower, and for everything they need.

Rebellion

The children grow up and become teenagers, and start rebelling. They stop thinking as their parents do and start thinking on their own. The 2-3 year-olds are going through this as well. They begin to assert themselves try to do things their own way. As the students begin to master the content, they start thinking on their own about how to apply the knowledge they've gained or the skill they've learned. They start doing things differently than their instructor has done.

Rebellion can be functional or dysfunctional. When it is functional, this stage can help them nurture their own ideas and find their own way forward. When it is dysfunctional, it neither supports them well nor helps them.

Results

The students see the results of the actions they chose to take.

Realization

Afterward, they realize how what they have learned can help them, as well as other people, achieve those same results again (if they are positive) or avoid those results (if the results were negative).

This 4R model is in use everywhere. I use it in my own coaching practice. Parents and school systems often teach kids according to the 4R model. They teach reliance on them to get information, rebellion is what is for 'me', results transact from what 'I' will get if I help or do something for someone else, and the realization is to know how to take care of others. They teach these things through the way they communicate.

It can be done in a functional way, and it can be done in a dysfunctional way, as well. On every single stage, there are different things.

I saw a lady one day. She was looking very nice and spoke very well. Her son got a little grumpy and stubborn about something, and she started pushing him away. She yelled at him and then, a minute later, was like, "Oh, it's okay. It's okay."

This is teaching the child something wrong. If you yell and push him away, let him cry. But because she tried to fix the mistake she made right away, he is not going to learn what mistake he made. She made the mistake of punishing him. First, you shouldn't punish. But if you do, let him realize he has made a mistake.

Instead, she didn't allow him to realize what he'd done was wrong. Within 90 seconds, she yelled, screamed and pushed him away, then reached over to comfort him and make him feel better. Because she doesn't give him time to get to the stage of realization, he doesn't complete the learning process. If the child never gets to the realization stage, the lesson doesn't get cemented in the brain and the learner keeps repeating the stages of rebellion and results.

Bennet, the founder of the (I.Q) test, spoke the same way, but his language was different. As parents, it's our responsibility with whatever we do with our kids to let them realize the mistakes they have made. Suppose the kid's reaction was the result of the book, he should be helped to realize why his mother yelled at him and why he was pushed. She didn't allow him to realize that. From my understanding, this is not really great parenting.

It sets the child up for failure later in life because you are not allowing him to learn the lessons. I was against the pushing, the punishment. If the child had done something, okay, he has done it. Let the child realize now. Kids are really smart. A kid will soon realize, "Now I can feel, really. Before, I was just thinking. Now I have had my own experience."

Kids are smarter than grown-ups. They can pick up on your emotions very quickly. Sometimes it seems like they can see what you are thinking. They have that much power.

Language Matters

"My words creating my world"

When we speak with anyone, how we use our words makes a big difference. Some people are very good at generalizing. They say things like, "You always do this," or, "You never do this."

Then, what happens? First, the person who hears these generalizations stops trusting you. Second, you irritate them. If someone does this with young kids, it can become a black-and-white belief.

We have discussed the role of language in one's life and how we can change someone else's or our own lives through communication. Now we will explore how action and thinking work together.

Its happen so many times, what we think, we do, and whatever we do, we think about it later. This is how action and thinking work. All psychological treatment models are based on this principle.

Here I will share with you two small stories. One of my close friends was learning how to drive a car. His instructor was teaching him, but my friend was not happy with his instructions because the instructor was using words which were making him fearful. He was losing confidence in himself.

The instructor was saying things like, "If you do not follow my way, you will fail." The instructor was also talking negatively about every single thing, saying, "You will fail."

For some people, this might be really good, because they take it as a challenge. However, for another person, it can have a very negative impact. The majority of the people don't like negative comments. In this case, my friend was losing his confidence and started using more negative words like 'It's very hard', 'I can't do it', 'It's going to take a long time', and so on.

Now, I will share with you another aspect of this. My friend and I were talking and he was sharing his whole story about what was happening to him. While discussing it, I asked him a few questions and then he decided to tell his instructor to let him drive, just control the thing if he did anything wrong. He asked this favor of his instructor and, on the next driving lesson, he was able to drive himself and also did a couple of practice sessions with one of his friends. After all this, his confidence levels rose and he got a driving license.

Here, we can understand how thinking affects our behavior and behavior affects our thinking. When our thinking, words, and actions are not congruent, there is a lot of frustration because not living an authentic life is very painful, just like procrastination. Now the real question is how can we become harmonious?

The first step is to build habits. Practice patience and delayed gratification. The second step is to use a language of possibility and probability. Avoid negative language such as the words 'can't' or 'never'. Third, understand the hierarchy of language and ideas. Take control of your ideas by taking control of your language.

In 1995, actor Christopher Reeves was thrown from a horse. He became completely paralyzed from the neck down. His skull was physically detached from his spine. Medical science said, "So sorry. There's nothing we can do. You'll die in the hospital."

He refused to accept that diagnosis and ended up getting treatment that was able to reattach his skull and his spine. He became an international spinal injury advocate. No doubt, he had lots of help, but the real help was that he kept commanding himself and communicating with himself in a positive attitude.

"No matter what people tell you, words and ideas
can change the world."
– Robin Willams

Chapter 5

❦ Physical Abuse - Change Your brain ❖

There are many types of physical abuse. 'Intimidation', such as standing over, looking down, or getting in a child's face or personal space and refusing to back off, is one type. Another is 'isolation', where a child's ability to escape from or abandon dangerous situations is limited. The third is a 'restraint', such as blocking a doorway, locking them behind doors, or tying them up.

Why Restraint Is an Abuse

If you are not allowing someone to explore the world, to explore their things, and are holding them back forcefully, what is that? To me, it is synonymous with abuse.

Restraint becomes abusive when someone is exploring something and is not allowed to do so. It's not just a physical abuse. It is a type of emotional abuse as well. It affects the child emotionally and psychologically.

This kind of restraint can create learned helplessness. It has an effect on the brain and the mind.

Caring is different. If a child is going to touch a hot wire or some electric stuff that will give them a shock, then restraining them is caring. You aren't doing it to stop them from exploring, but to prevent them from hurting themselves or others.

But if a child, around the age of 7 or 8, wants to explore something, and parents don't allow him out, they are forcefully stopping him. Kids want to go and buy something to taste, to try something different, and parents do not allow them to experiment. If something is dangerous, that's caring. If something isn't dangerous, it's helping a child explore other things. So allow them to explore and grow.

I'm not talking about drugs. I'm talking about things that won't harm them. Allow them to get a good experience of life. Tony Robbins actually did this with his kids. When his kids were growing up, he took them to a drug addiction center. He showed them what happens when people start taking drugs. They explored this and were able to see for themselves the results with a sane mind.

There's no need to allow them to take the drugs first and then have them find out. They can be shown the results beforehand. That experience will be more powerful than any words you could say.

Telling someone forcefully to stop, controlling their curiosity, that is abuse. Doing something when they are already scared won't help. Being a parent, we can assess and judge what is wrong and what is right. If there is something really wrong and your kid insists on doing it, educate them about it. Stay with them. Go with them if required. Tell them, "Look, I'll come with you. We can go explore this together."

Care about them, but don't hinder their experiences.

Aggression

The most commonly recognized form of physical abuse is aggression, such as hitting, kicking, punching, arm twisting, pushing, beating, shoving, biting, slapping, striking with an object, shaking, pinching, choking, hair pulling, dragging, burning, cutting, stabbing, strangling, and force-feeding. It also includes overdosing a child or misusing drugs to get them do what you want them to do. Endangerment, such as verbal threats of killing mixed with physical violence and use of weapons, is another type of physical abuse.

Spanking

Spanking is one of the biggest legal abuses. There are a few countries where spanking is legal, especially in developing countries and third world countries. The government doesn't have many laws to stop this. In Australia, spanking is not allowed, but parents still do it.

The purpose of spanking is to stop a kid from doing something. When you're physically hitting someone, it's going to cause them pain. They experience the pain and they assign the meaning of that pain to

"I'm not allowed to do that." It's going to impact their thinking. Physical pain alters thinking.

It isn't just the physical pain. It's the intensity of the experience as well. If the incident keeps repeating, it makes a big difference.

In some instances, it may seem the most effective way of letting a child know it is not okay to do something because it is dangerous to their health. A one-time incident may be important, especially if it relates to a life-or-death situation. However, there are other options available.

Sometimes it is a matter of paying more attention so that the child is prevented from being in that dangerous situation in the first place. Sometimes it is a matter of taking the time to make sure that potentially dangerous things are kept out of their reach.

Spanking will not increase their respect for you. It will stop them, but there are consequences to the health of their brain.

Spanking has a different criterion with different backgrounds. This practice varies culturally. In some cultures, it is approved. In some cultures, it isn't. The effect of spanking isn't bound only to the childhood, it tends to stay with the person all throughout his or her life. Sometimes kids say to themselves when they are grown, but this really happened before that.

I'll tell you about my incident. When I was very young, one of my cousins brought over a cigarette. He was a year older than me, and we were 12 or 13 years old at that time.

He showed me a cigarette because his father used to smoke. We decided to try it and started smoking. Another cousin of mine saw it and went to complain to my mother.

"Momma, he is smoking."

So she called me over and she asked me if I was smoking. I lied and told her no. So she told me to open my mouth and I had to. She smelled the cigarette smoke from my mouth and slapped me. After that, I never smoked again.

At that time, I was innocent and didn't know anything about smoking. I didn't know the consequences or how harmful it could be. I had no idea about the consequences. I smoked out of curiosity. She stopped me by using a negative punishment.

I always say thanks to my mom for that. It is because of her that I never smoked. That was part of it. The second thing was, my father never smoked either. He never smoked and never drank, and so he was a role model for me. I followed his example.

Also, it is important that the punishment is not given to the child when the parents are angry. It is important that the parents be in complete control of themselves when the punishment is administered so that it doesn't turn into abuse.

I was naughty, no doubt. I was kind of aggressive as a child too. I was a leader, and when I was a kid, if someone did something wrong to me, I was never scared of that person. If someone hit me, I was okay. But the next time, when I got a chance, I would make sure to hit the person back.

I'm not saying my parents should have encouraged this behavior, but every time I did something, my mother used to bash me. She never asked me what happened or why I did it. She simply beat me up for doing it. She didn't teach me a better way to handle things. Her only teaching was to beat me.

I'm not blaming my mother. She only knew one way to do things, and that was the culture in which she was raised. My mother loved me a lot.

The thing is, she would never beat me over other people's complaints. If someone came to my house complaining that her son did this thing to the other kid, she would not beat me over that. She would tell them to handle their children and she would handle hers, that was me. But when she actually saw me doing something wrong, she would beat me straight away.

My teacher used to spank me every day in place of teaching me properly. He had only one tool to teach me and every other kid in his class. What he did didn't help me to concentrate more on my studies. I was too busy being angry to listen.

Every single child has different psychological needs. Kids misbehave to fulfill their needs when they can't find healthy ways to get them met. Tony Robbins talks about the six different kinds of personality needs. These are different from the needs given by Maslow's hierarchy. These needs are - certainty, adventure, significance, love and connection, growth, and contribution. I have seen all these needs in the kids I work with.

The top 4 needs (certainty, adventure, significance, and love and connection) drive their behavior. Certainty and adventure will never come up together. One will come first. Once certainty is achieved, then the need for adventure will come up.

Let's look at a case of two boys. One boy is brought in for punishment because the teacher witnessed him hitting another student. Upon questioning, it is revealed that this boy patiently endured an hour of torment from that fellow student and warned him several times before finally hitting him because he didn't know how else to make the boy stop. The boy who hit his fellow student had a need for significance.

The other student is brought in for questioning and admits to tormenting the taller, larger student for an hour before being hit. That student's need was for adventure. He was curious what would happen, and the curiosity led to adventure.

Both students chose an unsociable and unresourceful way of fulfilling their needs. Tony Robbins talks about the different ways we have of meeting our needs: resourceful or unresourceful. Kids follow the same. They act to fulfill their needs. If they aren't taught resourceful ways, they will choose unresourceful ways.

If kids are getting their needs fulfilled, they aren't going to do the wrong stuff. But what happens? They don't know exactly how to fulfill their needs in a sociable resourceful way. Adventure - you can get that need met in so many ways. There's no need to bully someone. Bullying is making themselves adventurous and making themselves strong. Bullying makes you like a boss, like a mafia. Mafia is significance. I'm superior to you. Superiority is a negative way to get that need for significance met. The superiority of the leaders.

Leaders are superior too. But how do they become superior? They pick the right way to become superior. Especially in school, you can see the mentors, like some kind of heroes in the schools. Those are the kids who are always doing things the right way. Then people say, "He is a good boy."

I wrote about this a little - Good boys and bad boys. What about the bad boys? Why are they bad? They pick the unresourceful ways to make themselves feel significant or fulfill their need.

The thing is, we can associate all these things with kids who are abused as well. Although our main focus right now is kids, anybody can be abused in different days. Even the father or the mother in the family could be undergoing an abuse. Right now, though, my discussion about abuse is focused mainly on the kids and how it impacts their lives going forward.

When kids experience any kind of punishment or abuse, whether it is physical, emotional, mental, sexual, financial or spiritual, it has a negative impact on their lives. If we focus on the kids in the very beginning, they can have very good, happy, and healthy lives.

Chapter 6

❦ Sexual Abuse - Distortions ❦

"My fears of tomorrow are simply melting away."

Now I am going to talk about a very sensitive topic.

There are many forms of sexual abuse. Grooming, for example, can include doing an unwanted or embarrassing sexual act designed to catch a child off-guard and create feelings of trepidation (apprehension). It can also include exposing a child to sexually explicit content, such as pornography, in the hopes of desensitizing the child to such activities and getting them to accept that same behavior from the abuser later. This is known as destroying principles.

Molestation is the unwanted touching of private areas. This can happen when either the child is forced or encouraged to touch a person inappropriately or the person touches the child.

Sexual exposure happens when a person forces a child to look at his/her private areas while the person engages in a sexual act or when s/he forces the child to allow them to watch as they undress.

Rape is, by FBI's definition, penetration of the vagina or anus with any body part or object, or oral penetration by a sex organ of another person, without the consent of the victim. Many states acknowledge statutory rape, where sex with anyone under the age of 16 or 18 is considered rape since consent from children is not considered as true consent.

Another form of sexual abuse is sadistic sex. This includes immobilizing a child through drugs or alcohol and administering pain during sex, tying the child up, physically beating them, choking them, engaging in psychological torture, burning, cutting, stabbing, or murder before, during, or after sex.

Sexual abusers even use tactics such as threats where they bully the child into doing sexual acts with them by threatening to hurt someone they love if they don't obey. They also use fear tactics such as the threat of being left alone, hit, humiliated or punished if they don't comply.

The effects of child sexual abuse are devastating and can take a lifetime to heal. A third of those who experience it will end up committing suicide. A large percentage of them will become criminals or enter into prostitution. Almost all of them will experience relationship troubles throughout their lives.

Rape and Consent

Is a child ever able to give consent to sexual activity? No. Straightforward - No. There are lots of legal issues around this, which I am not going to get into, but consent means the child is old enough to understand what is right and wrong and is able to take the responsibility for the consequences of their actions.

In Australia, 16 is considered to be the age of consent. But if someone is significantly older than them, such as a 16-year-old boy or girl who is having sex with a 25-year-old woman or man, this is not a situation of mutual consent. This is abuse. The older partner is more experienced and smarter than their younger counterpart. They are much more aware of the results of their actions.

At 16, however, the child is still operating primarily on emotions. It will be a full six years before the brain is fully developed and conscious decision-making takes place. This is the biggest concern. How can the government allow this age as well?

There is no doubt that teenagers have a really big urge for sex. Many of them are heavily involved in sexual activities such as watching sexually explicit movies and pornography and some of them are starting activities that make them sexually excited such as masturbation. There is a curiosity there, especially about sex, but this is not promoted and not often considered a good area for conversation in many places.

In developed countries, especially in Australia, there is sex education in schools. However, there is no discussion about the emotional ramifications of sexual engagement. There is an explanation of how sex happens and encouragement to avoid pregnancies and STD's, but there is no explanation about the emotional, spiritual, and mental impact of having sex. Meanwhile, television programs groom children to begin thinking about and preparing to have sex at younger and younger ages.

Sex education programs in developed countries usually talk about the physical growth and the physical consequences, but they do not discuss the emotional consequences. In countries like India, however, there is no discussion about it at all. In my entire biology book, there was only a short discussion about physical development, but when it came to sexual reproduction, my teacher just told us to read it ourselves.

The social taboo was there, and because of that, the kids were getting their sex education from public toilets. Maybe a child goes to a public toilet and sees a picture of genitals inscribed on the wall and they become curious. They learn the slang terms for penis and vagina, and this is their introduction to sex education. Or they learn from their friends, who almost all have the wrong information.

Thus, the information they receive about sex is usually totally distorted. Because of this, such activities happen with mutual consent as well, even at their age, like two fifteen-year-olds.

I spent my teenage years in boarding schools. Boarding schools are celibate, but in those boarding schools, I heard lots of talk like this. Two boys, they were actually involved in such kind of activities. The mutual consent was there, but for what purpose?

This is why the term 'consent' is so dangerous. You can convince a four-year-old child to consent to many things. That doesn't mean they understand what they are consenting to.

When children are doing it in the same age group, we can guess that they are doing it with their own will and are experimenting out of their curiosity. With the same age group, they are not likely to do as much damage to each other, but still, it is not right.

Physically, they learn about that in school, but emotionally and psychologically, how much damage? That makes a big difference.

I spoke before about when I was in the boarding school. I noticed this. There was a grade 6 student abused by a grade 10 student. That had a really bad impact.

Two grade six students were playing with each other's organs and all this stuff, but it was out of curiosity. They had the same intellectual level and so they were not abusing each other. What they were doing wasn't right, I'm not promoting it, but we are talking about consent.

Those who are on the same intellectual level can give consent to one another. Neither of them knows more than the other about the consequences of what will happen as a result of what they are doing.

When one of the parties is more mature than the other, the less mature one cannot give consent. The older one is manipulating the younger one and taking advantage of the younger one's lack of knowledge. In this situation, how can the younger one give consent to the older one?

There are still plenty of questions about why all of this is happening, no doubt. There's an emotional part to it. Sex is not just a physical act. There is emotion attached to it too.

I watched a movie where some prostitutes made money out of sex, it was their business. Physically, they were involved with their clients, but they were not involved emotionally. They were involved with 4-5 men in a single day, but they didn't have any guilt over this.

If someone is in a committed relationship and gets involved in this, s/he can feel a guilt for that.

Girls sometimes commit suicide because they have been raped. Yet the prostitute, who sometimes has sex with 4-5 different men, isn't bothered by this. Why? Because she is not involved emotionally. The girl who was raped was not just attacked physically, but emotionally as well.

Sex is not just a physical action. It is an emotional action too. Kids, at the right age, should learn about sex from their teachers or the government or the community.

Why do people have sex in the first place? To satisfy their own emotional needs. They are looking to feel better about themselves or to feel good or for an emotional connection with others, even if they don't recognize that this is what they are looking for.

My way of thinking is this: Nowadays, especially the teenagers think that sexual activity is adventurous. And in many developed countries, it is treated as casually as a handshake.

There is a 22-year-old man on the social media who conducted an experiment to show just how vulnerable kids are. He contacted three girls, aged 12, 13, and 15, on the social media and talked with them. He was able to convince them to sneak out of their houses at midnight to meet him. Kids are taking sex very casually now. They have no thought about this, no concern at all.

The guy frankly told them, "Let's go. We're going to have fun tonight."

He had contacted the parents before he contacted the girls. He brought the parents to his van first so that they could see what was happening with their daughters. They put in the radios and cameras and he told the parents, "Look, your girls are going to come outside."

And the girls did. The youngest of them was just 12. Anybody could have kidnapped and killed her. Lots of such activities are happening these days. Not just in Australia, but around the world. Child trafficking is quite prevalent.

Those kids who were sexually abused at an early age suffer a lot mentally. One out of three of them will go on to commit suicide. This is a big number. More than 33% of them will kill themselves.

Out of the remaining 66%, many will become criminals and others turn predators themselves. They start doing it to other kids. Sexual abuse has a very bad impact on people.

"I thank the universe for providing me with opportunities to grow and to transform."

Chapter 7

⤛ Mental Abuse - Decide Your Future ⤜

"I am a stronger and wiser person because of my tests and challenges."

When a child experiences rage from a parent, caretaker or sibling, this is a form of mental abuse. That intense, furious anger which comes out of nowhere, usually over nothing, startles and shocks the child into compliance or silence.

Gaslighting is intentionally lying about the past to make a child doubt his memory, perception, or sanity. This, too, is mental abuse. It destroys his ability to trust himself and, just as importantly, to trust others.

The silent treatment is a punishment that includes ignoring the child and refusing to speak to them for long periods of time. The stare is when a parent, caregiver or the other person stares intently at the child with no particular feeling behind it or with obvious hatred. It is abusive because it makes the child feel intruded upon and uncomfortable.

Why The Stare Is an Abuse

It is the intention behind the stare that can make this abuse. When you are looking at a child, it creates a non-verbal reaction. It's a form of non-verbal communication. The child can understand the emotion behind the look. In the still-face experiments, there was no emotion and no intention to harm the child during the experiments. However, staring has emotions attached to it.

The definition of abuse is maltreatment. Staring makes people uncomfortable. When we are staring at a person and making them uncomfortable, we are not treating them right. We are maltreating them.

I saw in the families I worked with, how the stare affects children. When my son, who is just 3, is doing something and I stare at him, perhaps unintentionally, he puts his head down and looks around trying to avoid my eye contact. It is clear he is not comfortable with what I am doing.

Staring with the intention of stopping a child's behavior can be done very briefly, followed by a brief shake of the head, if verbally communicating with the child or explaining him/her isn't possible. However, staring at a child angrily is abusive. The intensity of the stare makes a difference.

I talk about this to let people know that it can make your child uncomfortable. It puts them down and causes them to lose their self-confidence and their self-esteem when we do such things regularly.

The intention behind the stare and the frequency with which you stare are the things that make the biggest difference in turning this into a form of abuse. A child may be doing something that, for him/her, is right and appropriate. But for the parents, they feel it is inappropriate.

For example, the other day I was in a restaurant with my son and my wife. It was his birthday, and he was playing around. He was jumping on the chairs and all around. I didn't stop him. He has a right to jump. My wife was looking at him. "Look at him. He's creating a mess."

I told her, "So what? He's not hurting anyone. Let him do it."

She was worried about what other people might think. I told her, "I don't care about other people think."

She told me, "They're going to think you can't control your kid."

I replied that he wasn't disturbing anybody. He was jumping on his chair and making a mess at his own table. She was so concerned about his behavior at that time and what other people were going to think about it. What happened?

Afterward, on the other side of the table, there were two ladies sitting. They started talking to him. When they did this, he came back and that was it.

Did he damage anything? No. I don't care about other people and what they think. I care about my son and how he needs to grow. If I am busy yelling at him to shut up and sit down quietly, what is going to happen? Next time, he is not going to do any activity with someone else. I am sending a signal to his brain that this activity is not appropriate for him. As a baby, in that situation, it's appropriate for him. If he were 8 or 9, it would be inappropriate.

At the age of 3, he has all the right to go do that. I don't want to stop him from that because he's just 3. He's more active than other people. It's good. I don't want to send the signal to him that activity is not okay, and then tomorrow, if I take him to the amusement park or something, he's not going to do anything there too.

I know that I need to help him think about whether this is the place to do this activity or not, but this is not the right time. He is 3. At this age, we can't teach him the difference between one situation and another. He has all the right to do whatever he wants to do right now. This is my thinking and my personal experience.

I have noticed this, especially in the restaurants and other public places, parents tend to teach their kids, "Do it this way," or "Do it that way." My main concern is to teach them the right way, but not stop their curiosity. My son is not like this all the time. But if he's doing that, I am not going to stop him as long as it is not disturbing anybody else.

Stopping him because I am worried about other people does not feel right to me. If I stop him, I want it to be for his own reasons. That's what's right. He should learn those things and manners, but not stop just because I am worried about what other people will think. No.

I have decided I am not going to stop him for anything unless it is really harmful or dangerous. Then, instead of stopping him, I will be with him to help him understand why it is not good. He goes with me more often than he goes with his mom because I don't stop him much. He listens to me more than he listens to my wife. If I say to my son, "No, we are not going to do this." He listens. And my wife complains that he does not listen to her.

I allow him to do things, he knows it and so he listens to me and pays more attention when I say something to him. That's really, for me, a personal thing. He knows I'm his father and I'm going to respect his curiosity and I'm going to respect his activities. I allow him to do things that he wants to do and he respects me for that. He knows if I say 'no' to something I will have a very good reason for that. We should respect our kids and their activities.

"I am superior to negative thoughts and low actions."

Why Silent Treatment Is An Abuse

Anyone who has had a teenager knows why the silent treatment is abusive. What do the teenagers do? They stop talking with their parents. And sometimes, parents stop talking with their kids.

"I'm not going to talk to you anymore."

I did this, actually with my mom once. I don't exactly remember the reason why I did it, but I stopped talking to her. What happened with me was, I was hurting myself every single day. I was sixteen at the time. I had to think about it whenever I would see her. And she did the same with me.

She tried to talk and I said, "I don't want to talk to you."

She told me, "Alright then."

It was a big lesson for me, and this is why I talk about why it is an abuse. It was hurting us both emotionally and spiritually. Things that hurt us emotionally stay with us for a long time.

Silence happens for kids in different ways. Isolating them, putting them in the corner, putting them in their room, locking them in their room, and we don't talk to them. It's all isolating them, and it's all a kind of abuse.

My main concern in this is how it affects the brain. When we stop talking to someone, how does it feel? Just feel it for a moment. You're feeling isolated. You are shutting down emotionally. You're feeling bad. It's hurting you in some way, it's overpowering your mind. This is why the silent treatment is an abuse.

Prolonged silence and isolation cause the neurons in the brain to shrink. It can cause long-term damage. Prisoners who have been put into solitary confinement for as little as two days have been shown to have long-term neurological damage from the isolation. Yet for an adult of age 20, 2 days is just a tiny percentage of their life.

This is why it is so important to be very careful just how long a child is allowed to be put into a corner or in their room or in any form of isolation. My definition of abuse is to mistreat and make people uncomfortable. The silent treatment definitely falls under this category.

Other Forms of Mental Abuse

"Behind every dark cloud, there lies a rainbow."

Projection is where parents dump their issues onto the child as if the child did it. Twisting is a form of this kind of abuse. When confronted about their behavior, parents twist the truth to blame the child for their actions.

Manipulation is making a child fear abandonment or rejection in order to get them to comply with something a parent wants them to do. This is never healthy. Last, but hardly the least, is the victim card. When all else fails, the parents act like they are the victims of the child in order to make them feel guilty and then they use that guilt to control their behavior.

Results of Mental Abuse

The results of mental abuse can lead a child to start smoking and drinking. Parents who neglect their children, don't take out time for them. What happens? The kid finds people who will pay attention to them, but those people often lead them in the wrong direction.

They start getting involved with kids who are engaging in risky behavior. They are not getting enough attention, love, and affection from their parents, so they look for it elsewhere. If your child is getting enough love and affection at home, they will not go looking for these in the bottom of a bottle or in someone else's bedroom.

I know through my own personal observation and experience that parenting is not easy. Lots of people become parents before they even know what the full responsibilities and expectations are. Many people have never had good parenting modeled for them. Parents who are aware, they need to become pro-active and learn what they don't know so that they can raise their child properly.

"All things are working for good in my life."

<h1 style="text-align:center">Chapter 8</h1>

<h1 style="text-align:center">✦ Verbal Abuse - Changes The Entire Life ➤</h1>

As we have already discussed, language is very important in the healthy development of a child. Verbal abuse destroys the self-confidence, self-esteem, and belief in their worthiness to be loved. It can lead to depression, isolation, and struggles with relationships that can last a lifetime.

Screaming, Yelling, and Raging

Extremes in volume and tone of voice is an example of verbal abuse. When an adult engages in yelling, screaming, and raging at the child, it breaks the child's trust in the parent and can create a fear-based environment where s/he lives fearful of the next time they will trigger their parent. Often, such extremes are accompanied by another form of verbal abuse, which is intimidating words. This is the use of swearing and threatening language that often comes when a child refuses or fails to do what a parent wants him/her to do.

Another form of verbal abuse is an intense manner of speech, such as being argumentative, demanding, interrupting frequently, talking over the child, withholding key information from him/her or interrogating. One more form of this is personal attacks such as criticizing, name-calling, mocking responses, defaming their character, berating their feelings or judging their opinions. It all leads to the child feeling insignificant, unimportant, and unheard.

Additional forms of verbal abuse are refusing to apologize, playing the blame game, and browbeating. When parents refuse to take responsibility and become hostile, invalidate or dismiss the feelings of the child, lie, and conveniently forget promises or commitments, this is abusive behavior. When anything that goes wrong is blamed on the child and the child is constantly accused of being too sensitive or the parents are overly critical of their reactions, this is abusive behavior too.

Finally, when parents say things like, "If only you would do this (or not do this), then I wouldn't have to be this way," or "You don't know how to take a joke," or "The problem with you is…" or "That (abusive incident) didn't really happen!" all come under this category.

Raising Your Voice

"My ability to conquer my challenges is limitless; my potential to succeed is infinite."

When you raise your voice, to what extent are you raising it? Kids have no criteria, no way to measure, to what extent you are raising it.

It's important, sometimes, to raise your voice. But not every time. When I compare the two countries, Australia and India, the developed and the developing, they have different cultural practices. But I have noticed one thing - when you raise your voice, it hurts. It hurts no matter where you are.

If you're raising your voice to get someone's attention or to stop them, it's okay. But yelling and screaming, blaming and complaining, these hurt.

Two years ago, I went to India. There was one man with a small child, maybe a year and a half old, and he was yelling at his child. We were in this big, crowded place. I don't remember the exact words he used, but I remember his expression and the way he was yelling at that child, that one-and-a-half-year-old baby.

Raising your voice can begin affecting your child even before they are born. Remember that learning and communication take place in the womb. How scary would it be to have that loud, angry voice coming through?

The words that child was hearing that day were like, "You are a monster! You can't do this or that."

I recall an incident that occured five years ago in Australia. I was in Big W shopping center with my wife and my son. There was a family with one child, maybe 4 or 5 years old, and his sister who was around 8 or 9. I don't know what she did to her brother. But the man, her father, he was a giant man. He was over six feet tall and would weigh 120 Kgs, maybe more. I saw him yell angrily at his daughter. People surrounding them were all looking at this, watching it happen. He was holding her hand and in her face and saying, "What's wrong with you? You can't see this?"

She was shrinking into her mother. Her mother was clearly so afraid and clung to her daughter. He wasn't loud, but the way he was talking was frightful. I was standing there watching and wondering what happened. I couldn't help but wonder at the way he was treating his own daughter.

Because of his activities, she's going to lose her confidence. She's going to lose her self-esteem. How is she going to react to other people in future? Because of him and his abuse. And I'm pretty sure it's not been the first time he would have done this. Looking at her mother, who was holding the girl, she did not say anything.

I can see this straight away. The man was clearly very dominant. He was controlling everyone around. The lady holding her daughter and both mother and daughter shrinking away from him. They were not talking, not even defending themselves. They were not putting their hands out and trying to say, "It's okay."

Maybe she did or said something to the three or four-year old boy, but it was nothing so extreme to deserve such a reprimand. The man should have talked to her and asked why she was doing something like that? He should have tried to teach her how to love her younger brother. But, no. The guy yells. That's one example of verbal abuse.

Verbal abuse is very damaging, and my whole topic here is communication. How we communicate. The tone makes a big difference, no doubt. Just a little change can impact someone in a big way.

When Your Child Won't Listen

Your children will become parents one day. They will learn how to parent from their own experiences, from how you parent them now. This is why I focus so much on how to treat your kids.

"You never listen to me!"

This is an example of a generalization, and parents tend to generalize a lot. The first thing I would recommend to the parents who struggle to get their child to listen to them is to stop reacting and start responding. When you are reacting, your verbal tone is very high and you're not using your logic and reasoning. Instead, your emotions are doing the speaking and this leads to words being said that you wouldn't say if you were thinking clearly.

Your reactions are based on what has happened to you in the past. You are reacting to that, rather than to the situation that is unfolding in front of you. Reactions come through your subconscious mind, which has no filter and no restraint. Responses come through the conscious mind and they have a filter attached to them that helps to stop you from doing real damage with your words.

Engaging In Conscious Parenting

To parents, I say: First, clear the past baggage which you are holding in your subconscious mind. The conscious building makes a big difference. Be conscious of your own behavior, about how you talk. Most parents are not conscious. They are just reacting on the spur of the moment. The reaction doesn't help. Conscious parenting can help.

Conscious parenting has different characteristics to it. It can play a big role in a child's development. Our language, what we use, and how we use it makes a big difference. Sometimes parents use very good words but the tone they use with the words does not match.

That makes a non-verbal impact. I asked some parents as I don't have much experience analyzing their thinking. When a husband and wife fight, the husband says firmly, "Don't do this." The wife gets it. Now, again, in another pair, the husband uses the same words but by yelling at her. It makes a big difference. The words you use may be good, but the tone you are using is not.

The same parents who complain that their kids aren't listening to them aren't usually listening to their kids. Children must be taught how to listen. They do not know how to do that automatically. If parents aren't modeling a listening behavior, the child doesn't know how to listen.

As an example of modeling in effect, I write in the mornings, usually before my son wakes up. But today, I was writing and my son came to me. The first thing he did was to ask me to come straight away with him, "Daddy, come. Come outside."

I told him, "Hang on. I'm writing something. Let me finish and then I will come."

He wouldn't let it go, "No. Come, come, come."

I told him, "Let me finish, and then I will come."

The second day, he came and did the same thing. He brought his drawing book with him this time and said, "Okay. Give me a pen. I want to make a drawing."

I gave him a pen and he began drawing. The same process went on for a couple of days. Today he came to me and straight away said, "Good morning, Daddy. Give me a pen. I want to write something."

What happened here? After a couple of days of watching me, he learned this. He modeled me. "My father is writing and if I write, I will be like him."

I appreciate him doing something. You do this, I'll do this, and we'll do this together. I finished my writing and he finished his drawing.

The first day, he interrupted me. The second day, he interrupted me. The third day, he drew and told me, "We have to do this first, and then we can do this together."

What we do models the behavior we see in our children. Tone affects them a lot. My son, sometimes, can't understand what my wife and I are discussing. My mind is very active, and I observe quite a lot. When something happens, I talk about it with my wife. I sometimes see an injustice happen, for example when I hear talk about sexual abuse, and I talk to my wife about it in the morning. My tone is high and excited. I am clearly upset about the topic.

What happens? My son starts talking. He thinks we are arguing about something. My expression is so intense and my tone so elevated that he becomes scared, thinking "Daddy may be angry." Then I have to reassure him that I was not really angry.

He couldn't understand my words, but he noticed my tone and the intensity of my expression. My wife was listening and responding nicely. My tone was high, though, because I was really upset about the things that were happening to these children. So my son tried to interrupt in order to stop the argument he thought was happening.

From the beginning, I noticed this, right after his birth. Whenever I would be talking and my tone would be high, he would start talking because he thought my wife and I were arguing about something. That tone had an impact on him. We were not abusing him, we were just talking amongst ourselves, but he thought there was something wrong.

Verbal abuse has an impact. Children are very sensitive to words, to tone, to body language, and to facial expressions. As parents, it is our responsibility to respect that sensitivity and to become more conscious about how we communicate with them. They are fragile. Our intense words and language can break them. The wrong thing said at the wrong time can have a lifelong impact.

Chapter 9

⟪ Emotional and Financial Abuse ⟫

"A river of compassion washes away my anger and replaces it with love".

Emotional and financial abuses are less recognized than physical or sexual abuse, but no less damaging to the child.

Emotional Abuse ■

When a child experiences things like nit-picking, where whatever is important to the child is minimized in comparison to the parent's agenda, or the parent belittles accomplishments, aspirations or a child's personality in front of others, and where teasing and sarcasm are used to degrade and mock the child, this is an example of emotional abuse.

Parents sharing private information without consent or exposing some shameful event from the child's past, along with constant reminders of shortcomings, usually in a passive-aggressive way, are another example. Also, when a child is questioned about every motive or move or about aptitude, this is emotional abuse.

Unrealistic Expectations ■

First, when someone is trying to measure up to unrealistic expectation others have for us, it can cause a feeling of unworthiness. We feel most unworthy when we are overwhelmed by an intense emotional feeling for one person and, due to a variety of reasons, feel that we just aren't worthy of that person's love and affection, if not respect and admiration.

When children are held to an unrealistic, unattainable or unsustainable standard and berated and treated as inferior on their failure to live up to those expectations, or when parents attempt to be the most important person in a child's life, these too are forms of emotional abuse.

When a child is treated as if the child was just an extension of the parent, rather than a separate human being with his/her own needs and desires or when a parent belittles a child's friends or other family members in order to convince the child those people are unimportant, this is a kind of emotional abuse.

Withholding love, creating a threat of rejection, or use of intimidation, threats, frightening behavior or destruction of treasured possessions are also forms of emotional abuse.

The symptoms of emotional abuse are increased anxiety, excessive guilt, insecurity, confusion, alienation, anger and fear, and hostility or even rejection. The emotionally abused child often has difficulty speaking up for him/herself or believing in his/her own self-worth.

Emotional Abuse Leads to Learned Helplessness ■

When kids are doing their best and loving their parents unconditionally, and the parents don't respond the same way, to one extent it is really good. They are teaching their kids to dim their intensity. Those kids can then generalize the same thing to other areas of life. When they do the same thing and don't get the same results, they are going to feel disappointed. The parents can teach them, early, in their home to prevent disappointment out of their house. When kids are disappointed at their home, they can handle this.

How it impacts them in the later stages, if the parents can never be pleased because the kids' efforts are not respected, the kids are going to eventually feel that there is no point in trying to make their parents happy. This will bring them to the same point of learning helplessness. They learn that it is a waste of time and it is not worth doing it.

Once they have reached such a point, what is going to happen? When they grow up and go out into the world, they are not going to show their love and affection to other people. They are not going to show their love and affection to their partner. Their relationships are not going to be strong because they are not showing their love and affection to their partner or their children.

First, this thing will affect the kids themselves. When they grow up, they will suffer. They will not show their emotions because the parents did not respect their intensity of love. Second, when they are not getting the exact response for their actions, they will channelize their love and affection towards something else.

It can go to any of the two ways, functional or dysfunctional. I have learned that when kids come in with anti-social behavior, this is one of the biggest reasons. They are not getting what they want from their parents, so they stray into wrong ways and wrong direction.

If they find the right way to channelize such things in life, they can benefit a lot. They can channelize it into sports or music. What happens if they devote themselves to these things? They are going to get more love and affection from other people, if not their parents.

There was a story about this in the book, The Boy Who Was Raised as a Dog. It was about a girl who didn't really receive the affection she needed. Her father left her family and her mother had four other children to raise. She was so busy that she didn't really have time to give the girl.

One of the neighbors started taking advantage of her, abusing her. She learned from that experience how to get more attention and affection. She started sleeping with other men as well. She learned to get the attention and affection she needed, not from her mom, but from the men who were actually abusing her. Her mother didn't respect her love and affection, and the girl chose an incorrect way to meet her needs. The doctor spent more than 2 years with this girl and was not able to get her out of this.

Shefali Tsabary wrote a book called The Conscious Parent. She talked about this as well. Parents must be conscious about the needs of their kids. Every kid has needs.

Unfair Comparisons

Let me share with you a case history which can provide some helpful lessons on this topic for us.

Marty is 25 years old now. I first saw him 8 years ago. He had very long hair, didn't speak to anyone, kept to himself, and spent most of his time listening to some kind of music. He kept gazing at the earth and walked slowly. He had all signs of someone who is depressed, but if someone took initiative, he interacted very well.

Since then, he has changed dramatically. He is now very active, has fun, and takes responsibilities and initiatives.

When I was talking to him, I gradually moved to his childhood and kept digging out his early experiences and learnings. He shared lots of funny and positive stuff, and then he also shared his beliefs which he had built during that time. He has one younger sister. She has been a slow learner, so there was no sibling rivalry.

He had a group and in it were three cousins and an uncle. They all used to play together. He was the youngest in the group. He always had this feeling that they were smart and intelligent, but he was not.

As you can see, kids compare themselves without knowing the complete picture or taking into account factors like age, gender, physical strength, and so on. It also came out that his group members were bullying him too.

Comparing the Past and the Present

I meet so many parents and have spoken to my friends about their childhood and rearing practices. I find that most of the time, they have very clear-cut answers and statements like, "In our time, there was no mobile, no internet, and no PlayStation. There were no computers and T.V had limited channels. Nowadays, kids have everything. They are very lucky to have all these gadgets. When we were kids, we had to work very hard to get even small things, but nowadays, kids get everything without much effort."

At the same time, they start boasting about their childhood, saying, "We used to go out and play with friends in groups. We used to play in grounds. It was a kind of freestyle life. There was friendship. We were so relaxed and our life was so easy, but now kids don't have many friends. Most of them are on social media and living inside the house. Most of them play solo games and they don't have an active, physical social life."

I wonder what they want to say because on one side they feel bad about their childhood and on the other side they feel proud. My point in saying this is to wonder 'WHY' parents compare their childhood with their children's. They know every day is a new day. Such comparisons make parents feel stupid and frustrated with their kids.

When parents provide everything to their children, they are making them dependent on them and setting a very bad example for future generations. Everyone knows the saying, "Too bitter and too sweet, can't be eaten."

In the same way, being a very nice parent or a very harsh parent doesn't work. Parenting is not a kind of mathematical formula or science equation. Parenting is an ongoing journey. It changes according to situation and time. We need to understand this simple principle. Stop comparing and start learning how we can contribute and add more value to our children's lives.

In this fast world, there are a few very important things to teach kids that parents must do as well. The reason behind this is it is very easy and effortless to teach kids if parents themselves are practicing something such as physical exercise, like going to the gym or reading a book every night before going to bed.

In the same way, we should teach our kids how to connect with the universe. Here I am not talking about the spiritual world, I mean connecting with the power of the universe.

We need to give feedback to our kids and teach them how to give feedback to other people like their friends, neighbors, classmates or teachers. We need to teach them how to appreciate and be thankful for the world in which they live.

Gratitude is a very important part of keeping a positive mindset. It helps to make a list of things to be thankful for at the end of each day. This can become like a prayer that is said before bedtime.

Financial Abuse

"I possess the qualities needed to be extremely successful."

Financial abuse can lead to many trust issues and financial difficulties down the road for a child. It is one of the least recognized forms of abuses.

Financial abuse includes a parent forbidding access to the child's money or possessions that were given as gifts, stealing from the child, defrauding or exploiting them financially. Demands that all financial gifts or inheritances be placed in the parent's name, or opening bank accounts, putting bills or credit cards in the child's name without their consent or knowledge, these are all examples of financial abuse.

Another kind of financial abuse is placing a child on a strict allowance with unreasonable expectations, setting them up for failure, punishing a child for spending his or her own money, and forbidding a child from earning money or receiving an education. These are all things that will set that child up for future exploitation by others.

When children are asking for money to buy something important and the parents don't allow them to, even though they have the money to do it, this is financial abuse. What happens? The kids will try to get what they need the wrong way. They may enroll in gangs and start stealing things to get what they need.

Chapter 10

⦉ Spiritual Abuse ⦊

'Creative energy surges through me and leads me to new and brilliant ideas'.

While there are healthy religious practices, religion can also be twisted and perverted into very unhealthy forms of abuse. As a friend of mine likes to say, healthy religion encourages Respect, Empathy, Love, Integrity, Guidance, Integration, Openness, and Nurturing. Unhealthy religion is full of Rigid Expectations, Legalistic Indoctrination, Growing Inconsistencies, and Overbearing Nosiness.

Here are some forms of spiritual abuse. First, dichotomous thinking where the child is taught to see the world in terms of those who agree with the parent and those who don't. The parent makes fun of, belittles, and shows prejudice toward others' beliefs. Similar, and usually related to this is elitism where the parents refuse to associate with people or groups they consider impure or unholy.

Submission is another form of spiritual abuse. Here the parents require the child to completely adopt their point of view, offering no room for differing opinions or questioning of their authority. The parents resort to name-calling, chastising, and silent treatment in order to gain compliance from the child.

The parents operate in a legalistic manner, where strict adherence to their rules and regulations are commanded with absolute statements about insignificant issues. They may demand blind obedience from the child to the point where they themselves are expected to be worshipped.

Another form of spiritual abuse is labeling of people who don't comply with their faith or beliefs. These parents teach their children that those people are disobedient, rebellious, lack faith, are demons or enemies of the faith. Estrangement from extended family members and friends outside of the religion, including practices such as shunning, alienation or persecution are often practiced when such labeling is dominant.

Parents may demand that the child demonstrates perfection and happiness at all times. Religious activities, such as attending the church, may have extreme demands, excessive expectations, and rigidity. This is known as a public performance.

Parents may abuse their authority, using their spiritual authority as justification for demanding that the child completely submits to them. They may also engage in fraud using their religion to cover up criminal misconduct or the transgression of themselves or others. This includes covering up sexual or physical abuse, financial felonies, and misdemeanors.

Spiritual abuse is very common these days. For example, I am from India so there are a lot of different religious practices, and I notice it a lot among the Hindu, Muslim, and other such communities. What the parents do is to tell their kids, "Let's go to the temple." They force them to go. They force them to follow some kind of religious beliefs.

That's one thing, and this is my main concern about it. I consider spiritual abuse to be forcing your child to follow some particular religion. I consider it an emotional abuse as well because when you compare your kids and say, "Follow this and you're a good kid," or "Follow that and you're a bad kid," that is a kind of abuse. They are damaging the core spirit by doing that.

Labeling Others

"I wake up today with strength in my heart and clarity in my mind."

Labeling is totally different. I have written more about in other chapters. When you put a label on someone, like a good boy/girl or a bad boy/girl, for example, it limits them. It tells them, "You are like this," or "You are like that." Putting a label on someone is like putting someone in a box rather than allowing them to go and explore more.

I can give you an example in psychological terminology. Someone is labeled as 'depressed'. What will happen? The person begins to think, "I am depressed." The label gives them a kind of brand. That brand can be bad or good. You are not allowing the person to live their life as it is. You are putting them into one or the other category.

There are lots of such people who have had a disappointment. They are suffering on the inside because of the labels other people have put on them and now they feel they have to live up to those labels. "Oh, he's a good guy. He can't do such things."

But they have had a lot of stress in their past and failing projects and they wonder what is going to happen with them. They worry that they are not going to live up to other people's expectations, and because of that, they suffer on the inside. That's what labeling does to people.

The Life-Long Consequences of Labeling

My neighbor is 74 years old. She has some negative beliefs about certain communities. It amazes me that at her age she can hold onto these negative beliefs. She has been through many different stages of life but is still holding on to that negative belief-set.

I try, sometimes, to figure out why she has these negative beliefs. Maybe she had a bad experience with those communities when she was younger and she allowed those experiences to drive her present behavior. It prevents her from being able to form healthy relationships with people in those communities, and this means she misses out on so many potential positive experiences.

Blind Obedience

Blind obedience is a big form of spiritual abuse. I have heard this more than 100 times. "Oh, my son or my daughter is very obedient. S/he listens all the time. S/he never does anything wrong. S/he is a nice girl/boy. S/he is an angel."

They do not understand that if this is the case, the child is not healthy. They are not thinking for themselves. They are teaching their children to be people pleasers who will do or say anything to make other people happy. This is dangerous for their emotional maturity.

When someone is a people pleaser, s/he feels frustrated inside. Such people feel guilty when they are unable to make other people happy. They feel guilty when they want to say no, so they say yes to things they really don't want to do just to make other people happy. They are not really assertive. It is hard to get someone who is a people pleaser to become assertive. These things are spiritual abuse.

Religious Background

I grew up in a house that had a religious background, but it was not high religion. My father was very neutral on this topic. I'm a Hindu but whatever we did with the religious stuff, we were not 100% about it. We were very flexible in terms of belief. We respected all other religions.

Those who do not respect other people's religions and have dogmatic thinking, that is where it becomes an abuse. Looking at everyone else and saying, "We are the best."

My mother is very spiritual, but not really religious. My father was the same.

I knew a few people who were very religious and didn't know much about other people's religions, yet they criticized them. These parents restricted their kids from being exposed to other people's religions and thinking. Religion is just a set of beliefs.

All religions have their own values, no doubt, and they help people in their everyday life.

For families who have a background in dealing with illegal stuff, fraud, and mafia or mob mischief, lots of spiritual abuse happens in such homes. The kids learn the same things every day.

There are kids who are behind bars because they saw and learned such things in their families. When they were interviewed and asked why they were doing those things, they said it was because they saw their parents do the same, and so, they started doing it too. Every time they blame their parents. What does this mean? They were abused in a very early stage.

Healthy Religion

"I am at peace with all that has happened, is happening, and will happen."

The first thing all religions teach you is how to build a good relationship with yourself. All religions are actually based on science.

I am Hindu. I know that yoga has shown scientific benefits. I used to have doubts and asked questions about why these practices were being done. Now I know there is science behind the religious practices. As I studied psychology, I discovered that every single religious practice was in some way related to human psychology.

Chanting and mantras have science behind them. The practices that bring families together, there is science behind that. The use of incense has science and logic behind it.

Religion is logical and scientific, but how people practice it is not always good. As a psychology student, I have seen that religion helps people to connect with other human beings, and it teaches them how to make themselves stronger. Even the small celebrations that religions do, nowadays people talk about that and how it is important to celebrate small achievements.

We follow, as Hindus, the Bhagavad Gita, and this was already mentioned there. Everything is there. What is the science behind that? Scientists now know that these small celebrations give reinforcement of positive things. When they receive the small celebration, it gives encouragement to look for more achievements.

Practices of gratitude, rather than harming people, are actually good for mental health. Focusing on the positive and learning to see the universe as working in favor of you rather than against you helps to keep you mentally strong.

I am neither fussy nor fanatic about any religion, but I can see its positive benefits. Every religion has basically the same set of rules with some variations because they are all dealing with human behavior. I go to many different temples. And I have gone to a mosque as well.

I have respect for every religion. I have questions about why certain practices are done, because in the Hindu religion – one of the oldest religions – we do so many things, but I always ask why we do it. It is fine to bring a child and teach him religion. However, when the parent is making the child do these things without allowing them to question or helping them to find answers, that becomes abuse. Without letting the child know why it matters or why it is important, it becomes abuse.

If the parents do not know what the importance of a certain thing is, they should seek the answers with the child. It is okay to admit you do not know, but find out! Otherwise, you might be encouraging your child to do something that is harmful to themselves or others.

We go to the temple, for example. What is the importance of going to the temple? God is everywhere. God is not just in the temple. What is the science behind that?

The science behind it is our intention. We make a goal to go there, and with our goal, we establish our priorities. We say what is important in our lives and what is not. When we go there, we may find 100 other people there. It is a social gathering. As we sit there, we recite the same songs and the same practices as others do. We gain from the collective energy of that place.

God is not just in that one particular building, but depending on what activities we do, it makes a big difference. Another point of gathering in the temple is to know that you are not alone. You are surrounded by reminders that other people are with you, believing as you do, going through the same things as you are.

You face a lot of opposition when you are trying to make positive changes in your life. You go there to the temple or the mosque or the church and you remind yourself that you are not alone, and you are encouraged by that reminder to keep going on this journey to become a better person and to continue working on your personal growth.

Otherwise, it is too easy to convince yourself that you are the only one dealing with the things happening to you. You can be tempted to give in and quit on your journey. Gathering together reminds you that you are not alone. Everyone deals with something.

But if there is no opportunity for children to question, to explore their religion and understand the religious practices so that they can make them their own, it is just a method of control.

"I am a powerhouse; I am indestructible."

Chapter 11

❖ Preventing Abuse ❖

'My future is an ideal projection of what I envision now'.

Prevention is the most important step, and it begins before the child is born. Educating yourself and informing others about the power of these influences is a key part of making sure those things don't happen to your child.

Studies have shown that when a woman is pregnant and is exposed to stressful situations, the shape of the brain of the child in her womb changes. The frontal lobe contracts and the more primitive areas of the brain expand. Those negative experiences in the womb do impact the child.

After Birth

Also, prevent something from happening by making your child aware of it. Build the confidence in your child that they can share with you everything that happens to them. Make sure the surroundings are safe for your child before you leave them there.

Get to know the people your child will be staying with. Observe how they behave. If something doesn't feel right, even if you can't pinpoint what it is, trust your instincts. Don't risk it out of concerns for making someone feel bad or because your child might be upset with you. Actions always speak. As parents, we have a sixth sense and we can tell whether things are right or not.

Be more vigilant. Parents can be more aware of things when they are dropping them off at someone else's house, even for 2 hours. Make yourself aware so that your kids do not have to go through any kind of trauma. Something happening to them, just once, can haunt their lives forever.

This is not a horror movie. When we watch those, we can say to ourselves, "It's just a movie." But no. This is really more than that. This kills people on the inside.

Resisting the Urge to "Shape" Your Child

Most of the parents I work with want to shape their child, but the way they shape their child is not healthy. They do two-twos, positive or negative. Positive rewards or negative punishments. If the child did something good, they will get a reward such as a lollipop or a toy. If they did something bad, they will get a punishment such as bashing or withdrawing from them.

There is a third way. This is a way to help them be confident and grow in their lives. The third way is to become involved with your kids. When you are involved with them, you will easily see how they can grow faster and quicker and how they can bond more closely with you.

This is my personal experience. My son just turned three a week ago. As a three-year-old, you might guess, he is very stubborn and can create a dramatic scene out of anything at any time, in any place.

He isn't burdened by worries about people judging him. He doesn't care what other people will think of him. He is living a totally judgment-free life. He isn't busy judging others and he isn't afraid of being judged.

One day, we were in the shopping center and he wanted to do something. I told him not to do it. He started crying and lay down on the floor, right in the middle of the shopping center. I didn't mind. People were looking at me, wondering what I was going to do to intervene. I know I am his father and it is my job to determine up to what level I should tolerate this behavior.

I decided to lie down with him, right there on the floor, and within one minute, he sat up and was watching me. The temper tantrum stopped. My son finally learned and he is with me right now. When we work with the kids together, they grow more awesome. Involvement is the third way, and it is the real power.

Addressing Child Care

"My efforts are being supported by the universe; my dreams manifest into reality before my eyes."

Children in developed nations often go to childcare. There, they learn many things. They do physical activities with a fence, which helps them. What's the problem there? In the childcare, the caretakers often use the wrong language.

To demonstrate this, I will tell you a story. One day, I was with my two-and-a-half-year-old son. I opened up something and he said, "What's wrong with you?"

I started thinking to myself, "He's two-and-a-half years old, and he's using such language with me. What's he been learning? There's something wrong. He shouldn't be saying things like that."

But he learned such language from his caretakers at the childcare center. I talked to them about this.

That's the thing. We have to be very careful. Physical moments can change your brain and the language learning as well. Practice conscious awareness. With the conscious awareness of how you talk and how you interact, we can help the kids.

Listening Is Involvement

Children do not have a filter on their feelings. As a result, they 'feel' things far more intensely than an adult. For example, a young boy of age 5 falls madly in love with a girl in his kindergarten class. He talks about her all the time.

Many parents want to shut down that conversation. They tell the child, "You are too young for love," or "You don't know what love is." They insist the child stop talking about the girl. And the boy does stop talking to his parents about her. But that early experience of being shut down and repressed results in his withdrawal, emotionally, from his parents. He won't be talking to them when he is a teenager either.

Suppressed feelings create lots of issues. When feelings are suppressed, it is a big emotional trauma.

Being involved with your children, being part of their journey, means listening to them and taking them seriously. These little ones can have big feelings, and it is important not to forget that.

Healthy Parent-Child Relationships

There is not a fixed dimension of a healthy parent-child relationship. There is no magic recipe. It takes awareness and education. These are the keys to creating a healthy parent-child relationship. A healthy relationship has parents strongly bonded with their children, and children strongly bonded with their parents.

There is a respect for one another. They listen to one another. They understand the difference between good and bad. This is the basis of a good relationship, in my opinion.

Avoiding the Good Child/Bad Child Trap

It is common in society to praise children who behave the way society expects them to and to punish those who don't, but this leads to problems later in life. When negative emotions such as anger, fear or jealousy are not given positive outlets or means of expression, they can become toxic and lead to a child who can't even acknowledge that s/he feels such things out of fear of rejection or punishment.

"The human mind's capacity for self-deception is infinite. People who believe in pure goodness are capable of the most unscrupulous evils. Outside of our awareness, our lesser qualities express themselves through our unconscious behavior."
– Scott Jeffreys

When we teach children to repress negative emotions rather than helping them to understand both why they exist and how to direct them in a positive way, we lead them to develop a shadow-self that, unacknowledged and hidden, does terrible things to themselves and to others because of those negative emotions.

Striving To Be Good

How do we define the difference between good and bad? This makes a big difference. What may be good for one could be bad for another, and vice versa.

If I do an action, and I get the result I am looking for, out of that action, I am likely to think of it as a good action. However, good actions must not hurt me, they must not hurt my family, my community or anyone in the whole world. If it hurts no one and benefits someone, it is a good action. If it is good for myself, good for my family, good for my community, and good for the world around me, it is a good action.

If something is just good for me and it is not good for my family, community or the world, it is not a good action. It is a very competitive world nowadays. Taking steps forward in my business might seem to hurt my competitors, which would make it bad, but it is going to benefit my family and my society. It will benefit my competitors in the long run because my success will challenge them to improve their service and their products and they will grow from the experience as long as I am competing in the right way.

Self-Deception and Rationalization

We deceive ourselves and rationalize bad behavior to convince ourselves that it is a good behavior because we want to be right. We have rules about what we are supposed to do and what we are not supposed to do. Everyone has their own rules about this.

And when we want to do something we know breaks those rules, we may choose to deceive ourselves and rationalize that behavior in order to continue feeling good about ourselves, even though we are doing what we know is not a good thing.

We make these rules on the basis of our past experiences. We want to prove ourselves right and good. This kind of behavior is a big evil. It is a refusal to acknowledge that we are doing something wrong.

Ego gives the logic for why it can be done and still be okay, but inside, we know it isn't really good. If it were good, we would not need to work so hard to find the logic that would allow us to break the rules. On the basis of our experiences, we give the logic. According to our rules, we are right. Knowing what action we are trying to give logic for, is helpful.

When we are talking about abuse, this is especially important in their family and relationships. When they grow up and there is some kind of dysfunction between the husband and wife or with partners, at that time, the rules come up. They start giving their logic.

For example, there are two partners, and one of them is saying, "She's a woman. She shouldn't share like that." This is a rule he grew up believing was true. On the basis of his own personal rules, he was talking like that. He made his rules based on his personal, past experience and his knowledge. This is the reason such discords happen.

Confronting the Dark Side

Blaming other people and not taking responsibility, the victim mentality, is growing nowadays. Every human being has a shadow identity and a good identity. How and what you feel makes a big difference. Situations happen. A nice, good man who never thought about doing such kind of things can become a criminal or even rape someone when triggered in such a way.

Triggers make a big difference. Social media is one of the biggest triggers today. So many things are available so easily. You can watch porn easily online now. On Facebook Live, people are doing sexual activities and sharing it with each other.

There are right uses of technology. But just as many people are using technology in the wrong ways. It's very handy and very easy. The handier and easier it is, the easier it becomes to do the wrong things with it.

The greatest danger is being unaware of your dark side. If you know you have a dark side and you are aware it exists, you will be vigilant and on the lookout for it to show up. If you don't, that dark side can persuade you to do all kinds of harmful things. Human beings are masters of rationalization and self-denial. We are capable of justifying any kind of evil we can think of doing.

A friend of mine likes to say that denial is a really big river that runs through the state of confusion. Everyone takes a dip in that river from time to time, but it's never wise to go out there and build a houseboat and live on it. Denying what you are capable of doing is the fastest way to find out your limitations.

If something has happened to you in the early stages of life, it can produce such a shadow inside you. You can heal the pain from what happened to you in the past. The first step is to acknowledge what happened to you. Acknowledge the situation.

The healing steps are self-hypnotism, affirmations, and speaking with a professional as well. My main focus through this write-up is coming to a point where, when we are aware of all things and how these damage people, as parents and as responsible citizens of the Earth, we should look after the kids the right way.

Chapter 12

⋘ Addressing Abuse ⋙

"Happy thoughts Bring happy things"

While these chapters provide a starting point to talk about abuse, it's by no means exhaustive. Abuse can happen in a variety of ways and, sadly, abusive people abuse their creativity to come up with new ways to abuse others every day.

This list was initially provided by Christine Hammond, a Licensed Mental Health Counselor and a National Certified Counselor, who lives in Orlando, Florida and is the award-winning author of The Exhausted Woman's Handbook.

Listen To Your Kids

Make sure that your kids know you will listen if they do talk to you. If they aren't confident you are going to listen without judging them, or without doubting them, telling someone you've been molested is not an easy conversation to have. If they don't trust you, they aren't going to open up and admit that it happened to them.

Second, if something happens in spite of all that, listen to your child. Support them. Acknowledge them. Be with them. Do not respond, "Don't tell anybody that this happened to you." This is not a good way to respond.

Many people have written that they had something happen to them, they told their mother, and it was their mother who told them, "Don't tell anybody." This is especially the case if it was committed by a family member or a close family friend. The other relatives can actually shame the child into not speaking up for themselves.

This is a very bad practice. When ignoring what happened, even when it is done by a relative, the abuser is encouraged to continue. "No one's going to speak out against me. No one's going to stop me."

That kid, who is abused, may then grow up to abuse others, confident that nobody will stop them because they didn't see their abuser being stopped. This needs to be talked about, and abusers need to be stopped so that they can't do more damage to someone else.

The silence must be broken. Promote your children. Support them. If you won't support them in this kind of situation, you will never be able to win their trust.

Harish Iyer is a very famous guy in India and he narrated his own story about his childhood sexual abuse experiences. When he was 7, his uncle began abusing him. He told his mother, but she never stood up for him. For 11 years he endured that abuse and not just with his uncle, but with his uncle's friends as well. Now, he speaks out against it and there have been two movies made of his autobiography.

He went to the public to tell what happened to him. So, never shut anyone's mouth. Encourage your children to talk. If someone is suffering already, they should be allowed to share it. They should feel free to share with their family that it happened to them so that it doesn't have to happen to someone else.

More than half of the population has experienced some form of abuse. Physical and sexual abuse cause some of the biggest traumas because lots of social concern is attached to these. In society, we don't bother much with the mental, emotional, financial, and spiritual abuses. But sexual abuse causes a big trauma, and the community and society do not encourage talking about it.

Seek Healing

"I am blessed with an incredible family and wonderful friends."

Be sure the child or the adult victim gets healing. There are lots of studies that have been done on people who come from abusive or dysfunctional families. Their relationships will be damaged in the future as well. They can't focus. They can't trust. Their ability to succeed in life is greatly damaged.

When the people you are supposed to be able to trust prove untrustworthy, you grow up not knowing whom to trust or how to trust. That incident remains in their mind, affecting them. Sometimes they doubt themselves, sometimes they don't value themselves so they allow themselves to be used and mistreated by others just for the hope that someone will love them.

They feel worthless and this drives their behavior down a negative pathway that is very difficult to overcome. If it is just one incident, a person can recover more quickly and more easily, but children who suffer from long-term abuse like this have a very difficult time overcoming that past history.

Where Abuse Begins

Abusers have been through their own things and their own traumas. Based on their past experience, they made these rules. If something doesn't match up with their rules, they start getting angry and illogical. They become stubborn and defensive of their rules.

Based on their past experience and their knowledge, they generalize these things. When we start generalizing, it is actually a big deal.

There was a study of those who were involved in criminal activities. Most of the people who end up in prison, they discovered, were abused in childhood. It was shocking to me. However, if someone is abused in early childhood, they can end up doing the same crimes and becoming an abuser to someone else.

It goes back to parental modeling. If you've had someone abuse you, that is all you know. That's the only way you know to connect with other people or resolve conflicts. I was listening to Harish Iyer and he went to Riverside. He was abused there, but instead of becoming an abuser, he became an activist against abuse. He took that pain and found a resourceful way to use it. He thought, "I've been through this. How can I help stop someone else from having to go through it?" He learned a different model – how he could break the cycle.

Abuse is a mental disease in our society. It has been happening for centuries, and it is largely unrecognized as a disease and untreated. It has not been cured properly, which is why it is still prevailing in society. Like any disease left untreated, it is spreading.

In Australia, there was a child world commission. I just opened their website and listened to them. They had some kind of event on Arbor Day, but otherwise, people don't know they are there. 10% of the population, perhaps, knows about them. What about the rest of the population?

In the schools, they are teaching different things than they are teaching on the website. They are talking about the causes. Don't worry about the causes. Worry about the prevention and the treatment.

Talking about what causes people to do this doesn't help anybody. What are they making people do now? Sexual abuse. It's only going to help when you teach kids how to face the situation. Educate people who are suffering in how to get treatment.

I don't know if I'm really stupid or smart, but I'm starting to wonder what is going on. Why aren't we reaching out to the 90% of the population and educating them? Studies tell us that the criminals in our society were abused.

What are we doing about this right now? We are waiting and watching. We wait until they abuse someone else or commit a crime rather than helping to identify and treat their illness. It is important that abuse is addressed and healed so that those who are abused do not go on to become abusers.

Bullies

"Though these times are difficult, they are only a short phase of life."

To cover the topic of bullying, we would require a whole book. Bullying is not a new thing. It is an old practice. Bullies change faces all the time. Nowadays bullies use technology.

I shared with you what happened in boarding school and that was a form of bullying. If something was intense and it impacted my emotions, that's bullying. Bullying can have a really bad impact.

The victim of the bully can have their psychology changed by the experience. There are lots of games for bullying and people killing themselves as well. There's a Blue Whale Challenge that is going around right now. It's a "game" of challenges spread over 50 days. Lots of kids have killed themselves as a result of this challenge. They designed that game in such way that after someone has been calling them and bullying them, they commit suicide.

Why kids get bullied?

This is because the parents are not really aware. Most of the kids who get bullied don't have very good relationships with their parents. Maybe financially it is a very good relationship where, whatever the kid asks for, the parents provide. But the trust and emotional bonding are not there.

If something bad is happening with the kids, they must share with their parents. Parents have to listen to whatever their child has to share. Sometimes the kids are a little naughty, and the parents don't trust them. Bullying is growing because the relationship between the kids and the parents is not really that strong.

Those kids who have a good relationship with their parents, when they get bullied, they let their parents know. The parents talk to them and empower them by letting them know how to handle it. They talk to the teachers and the support network.

Parents have a responsibility to empower their kids. They also have a responsibility to build a good, trustworthy relationship with their kids so that they can help them.

I talk about this and I teach students how to handle bullying. I talk about awareness of bullying to kids and to parents. This is a big part of the relationship between the kids and parents and between the kids and the teachers.

Bullies are not just in schools. They can be anywhere. Even a teacher can be a bully, and bullies can be in the home as well. They can be siblings, parents or neighbors.

Recognizing When You Are the Bully

The problem with bullies, though, is that they don't see themselves as bullies. They may consciously know they are doing something wrong, but they justify what they are doing. Parents are sometimes bullies to their kids. I mentioned in an earlier chapter on abuse about a big man, holding his little girl's hand and yelling into her face, "You stupid idiot!" That was bullying.

In the big shopping center, he was doing that to her. He was maybe 40 years old and 6 foot tall. He understood what he was doing. But if someone were to ask him, he would justify the action. That justification is the problem.

There's no easy way to get people to recognize when they are being the bully. Every single sentence has a different meaning. The same sentence may be easy for you, but for me, it may be hard.

The simplest way to get someone to confront the fact that they are bullying others is awareness. Educate them about what constitutes bullying at a time when they are calm. Then they would be happy to listen to someone and understand the reasoning behind it.

If you want to try and educate someone who is already on fire and angry, be ready for a big fight. S/he will justify his/her behavior to you. For example, if I had walked up to that man who was yelling at his daughter, he would have fought with me. He would not be willing to listen to me.

Once he has calmed down and I talk to him, he might be open to listening to me and this is the way we can get through. But to try talking when they are emotional or angry, it is not going to work.

I noticed this even with one of my good friends. She is, to me, spoiling her kid. I have talked to her, but she tells me she knows what she is doing and that she is doing very well. And it isn't just me. Other people can see it as well that she is spoiling her child. I really wonder why she does it, but I can only guess. She's not my client, so I don't know exactly.

That's the problem, but education and awareness can make a big difference. This was not my case, it was someone else's, but I brought it up here because it is relevant.

One man, who has a daughter said, "I don't want another child. I don't want to share my love with anybody else. I just want to give everything to my daughter."

It's great that you want to love your daughter, but the thinking behind it about your love and affection is not really great. The thinking is going to spoil your daughter.

"I want to give everything to my daughter."

What do you mean by everything? Maybe you can give her all the money and everything, but your 'emotion' is what she really needs, not more than that. You give her more than that, it's going to spoil her. That's the thing.

With the bullying, the same thing happens. People try to protect someone, and they do it in the wrong way. But bullying is not really my kind of thing. I don't know much about it. I do know it has a very bad impact on people. It affects them psychologically and emotionally.

Carl Jung wrote about inferiority complex and superiority complex, those who believe they are worthless and those who believe they are above everyone else. But a complex, in my opinion, is a complex. The person who feels the need to prove him or herself to be better than others, it means they have an inferiority complex.

The Bully Complex

Bullies are insecure and always feel that way. They are trying to make themselves feel significant. They want to feel more powerful and better than other people around them. That's the problem, and that's why they are bullying.

They tell themselves they are feeling really good, but they don't have love for themselves. That's the problem. They are seeking affection, they are seeking significance outside of themselves and that is the problem. This does not just refer to the bullies who are kids but refers to bullying in all relationships. If there's abuse in a relationship, these are the things that can happen to you.

Husband and wife, they abuse each other. Verbally, they bully. Nagging at each other, putting each other down. For what purpose? They have a complex. They are looking for ways to make themselves feel important.

I noticed once, a long time ago, while sitting in a party, that there was a guy talking some negative stuff about his wife. He was nagging her in front of everyone. Why? What was he looking for out of this?

If we are friends and we say these things to one another when we are alone, it is okay. But in front of other people, what is the point? The lady got very angry that day. She didn't say anything but you could see it on her face.

Why do that? She's your partner. You should respect her. He put her down in front of other people. Maybe, I'm just guessing, when they got home, they had a fight. He insults her in front of all those people just to make himself feel like he is better than her.

Complexes have no age limit. It is inside every person. It can be a six or seven-year-old, or a 70 or 80-year-old. Everybody has the same thing. They can use it in a positive way, but bullying is bringing it out in a dysfunctional way.

Putting other people down is unhealthy and dysfunctional. Most of the time when bullies put people down, they do it in front of other people. This is my thinking. There are lots of theories behind it.

I acknowledge my own self-worth; my confidence is soaring.

Chapter 13

⋘ Healing From Abuse ⋙

"Creative ideas just flow out of my mind naturally "

For those who have been negatively influenced because either their parents didn't know or they didn't know, there is hope. The brain has demonstrated a remarkable plasticity, or an ability to reshape and reform itself, even in the adult years. Language is the key to changing the damage that has been done and reclaiming those areas for ourselves.

Increase Communication Skills

Emotions can also change things. Using intelligence tests that test for verbal and non-verbal skills, we can find out which thing the person or kid is lacking. What psychologists then do is focus on that particular area. If it's verbal, they talk to the parents and encourage them to sit with their children and talk to them. Give them a chance to grow.

What happens? We monitor for the impact on the right and left hemispheres of the brain, and it changes. With the improvement of the language skills, the performance goes up. If something has already happened or is damaged, we can change that, we can replace that.

To illustrate the truth of this point, I will tell you about my friend. When her son was just 2 months away from turning 8, he stood in her bedroom telling her not only that he was going to kill himself, but exactly how he was going to do it. And he had a backup plan in case the first plan didn't succeed.

She didn't realize until later how unusual her reaction was, but instead of blaming her son and asking, "What's wrong with him?" She thought to herself, "My son didn't come into this world broken like this. What did we do to break him?"

As parents, she and her husband began a journey to search for what they were doing wrong and to figure out how to fix it. Their communication skills at the time were very poor. Their conflict resolution largely consisted of yelling, screaming, sometimes throwing things, and occasionally punching walls. The unhealthy backgrounds in which they'd both grown up hadn't given them the tools for successful conflict resolution.

This, along with other problems that came from their dysfunctional relationship, had the child feeling trapped in a cage of fear with no obvious escape route except death. He was so afraid of change that he refused to try anything new and would panic when things did not go exactly as planned.

Now, that child is 21 years old. Because they recognized the problem and began working to fix it, as soon as they did, he became a reasonably healthy and mostly happy adult. He is now self-sufficient and while he still struggles with occasional bouts of depression, he is not on drugs, not addicted to alcohol, and is well on his way to success.

Lots of work has been done on the subject of neuroplasticity, and it is still going on. Physical therapies, psychological therapies, and child development psychologists are pretty much the ones doing the work on this, trying to understand how to help those kids who have been negatively impacted by ignorance or neglect.

People can do this in their own homes too. There is only the need to understand the right way to do it. I want to send this message around the world so we can wake up to what's happening to our children because of our mistakes as parents, in what we are teaching our children.

Detecting Early Childhood Trauma

My friend has a clear memory of the day her son told her he was going to kill himself. It imprinted itself on her brain in a way that she will never forget it. To this day, she can remember exactly where she was standing when it happened.

Her son, too, can remember it. For her, it was shocking. But she was an adult. She went through it with an adult's ability to reason and to think through the situation. For her son, as a child, it had a much more lasting and negative impact because he didn't have the communication skills needed to correctly understand and interpret his experiences.

She has already done a very good job correcting the problem. He is 21 and sounds like he is doing very well. But the fact that he still struggles with periodic depression means there is something he still needs to address. He is away from her now and so it is up to him to find out what the source is and deal with it. Until he does, that thing will remain in his subconscious mind and will determine his future.

The subconscious mind is a million times stronger than the conscious mind. 10% of your brain is under the control of your logical, analytical systems. However, 90% of your brain functions are ruled more quietly by the subconscious mind. When there is an early childhood trauma, such as my friend's son, depression, suicidal tendencies, and feelings of hopelessness or helplessness often emerge. These are strong signs that there is a past memory operating in the background that is causing problems and needs to be addressed.

The Psychological Tools To Heal

Psychology provides many tools to help those who are dealing with past traumas. Therapy is one such tool. There are many different ways that therapy can help, both verbal and non-verbal. The verbal therapies can teach a patient how to communicate. The non-verbal therapy focuses on helping parents to bond with their kids.

When we focus on helping parents to bond with their kids, the child's performance gets better. Intelligence can be identified. Bonding creates a more positive response to things. Emotional bonding is a very powerful tool for helping someone grow in a healthy way.

It wasn't until my friend and her husband learned to improve their communication skills that they were able to break through their son's resistance and prove that they cared about what he thought and what he felt and if he expressed those things to them, they were going to take action to help him resolve whatever problem he faced. That started building trust. By the time the child was into his high school, they had a really good relationship with only a few instances of rebellion on his part.

Overcoming Abuse

Abuse doesn't really need to be overcome. Which kind of abuse is the easiest to overcome depends on the person who underwent it and what kind of impact it had on his/her life.

Some people who have been through the abuse are going to tell you how it was to go through life without money. That was a big abuse for them, and they never forget about it. Tony Robbins always talks about his father and how poor they were growing up. Oprah Winfrey talks about the sexual and financial abuse she went through. She's never forgotten those things.

Abuse does not happen in isolation. Abuse is not just physical or emotional and that is it. These are interconnected. Physical abuse can cause emotional, mental, and spiritual abuse. Financial abuse can cause physical, emotional, mental, and spiritual abuse. Sexual abuse is a type of physical abuse and even it causes emotional, mental, and spiritual abuse.

So abuse does not have only one type of impact on the person's life. It can come with multiple impacts on all areas of their lives. We are not just physical beings or mental beings or emotional beings or spiritual beings. We are a collection of all these. An abuse in one area of life impacts all those areas of our lives too.

Thus, how easy it is to heal an abuse depends entirely on the person who is abused and how well s/he can adjust afterward. The type of healing they seek and how quickly they seek matters too.

Depression and Abuse

When some kind of trauma happens, such as a sexual abuse, the person who has been abused often feels like there must be something wrong with them. If not healed, they will always think that they are worthless and something is wrong with them. They will lose confidence.

This is why one out of three who are abused, commit suicide. Studies have been done on this.

Forgiveness

Many abusers end up abusing others because they will not forgive the person who abused them. They hold onto that anger, and it takes control of them. When we do psychological interventions, using the timeline technique, we do the same thing. We make the person, who is struggling, go back and forgive the person who hurt them.

When they do this, initially they feel associated with that person and event. Afterward, they feel disconnected from that event as well as the person who hurt them. When they disconnect, they feel relaxed and empowered to let go of the pain of the event.

Forgiveness does not mean that the thing that happened was okay. It was not, and never will be. What it does mean is that you acknowledge that the person who hurt you was in some kind of pain and s/he tried to fix that pain by passing it on to you. You refuse to accept that burden because it doesn't belong to you, and you don't want to pass it on to others. So you let it go.

When you can forgive, you can also acknowledge the good characteristics of the person who hurt you rather than just remembering the negative ones of them. Every abuser has something about them that is good.

Developing Self-Acceptance

Alexis Marson, LMFT, a psychotherapist who specializes in working with individuals, couples, families, and children, has a lot to say about the importance of self-acceptance and how to develop it.

He explains that this inability to accept ourselves comes from a combination of scarce self-knowledge and wounds from our past. It can keep us from developing authentic and healthy relationships with others.

Marson recommends several strategies to help you or your child, whoever is struggling, in the quest to develop self-acceptance:

First, learn to be vulnerable but with safe and supportive people. Choose an environment that gives you a safe place to open up about your vulnerabilities and people who will accept you for who you are, where you are, and exactly as you are.

Second, accumulate self-acceptance resources such as books, audiobooks, videos, and other positive tools. These can help you build up a belief in yourself and an ability to see your true value.

Third, revise the stories you tell yourself about your worth. According to Raquel Kislinger, Marriage and Family Therapist, MA, LMFT, "It is important to look at the stories we tell about ourselves, and ask if they reflect our hopes and dreams; if they bring us a sense of contentment and equilibrium; if they nurture our strengths; if they 'work' for us and are the tales we'd like to carry forward."

If not, we should work to rewrite them in a more positive way. Find the exceptions in life that allow you to reframe the story in a positive light. For example, a man holds a life narrative that he's clumsy and can't handle anything fragile. He's also a bad teammate because he fumbles the ball. He's never invited to events because he bumps into people.

"If we represent that person's life as a long succession of events, we might, indeed, find ones that support his problem, the story of 'clumsiness'." Kislinger said, "But we'll also find exceptions, which help to create an alternate, supportive story such as: catching a fly ball at a baseball game; receiving several invites to parties; safely transporting a glass vase during a recent move."

Let yourself feel all your feelings.

Alexis Marson also specializes in helping people remove the obstacles to self-acceptance. In an article titled 'Why We Can't Accept Ourselves – And Small Ways To Start', "True self-acceptance involves all emotions - joy, rage, terror, sadness, elation, etc. Feeling all these gives the process of self-acceptance more momentum."

Her method starts with helping her clients begin connecting with what they're feeling using a visualization technique where they mentally imagine themselves being scanned and then describe anything they notice in each of the areas of their body. Once they can identify the symptoms of the emotions they are feeling – such as sweaty palms, or a racing heart, or other things that might indicate anxiety, fear or worry, she can then begin to help them accept those feelings and the messages being sent to them.

Dr. Susan Jeffers said in her book, <u>Feel the Fear and Do It Anyway</u>, that there are three levels of fear. She concluded that at the bottom of every fear is the greatest one of all: the fear that you can't handle it. The truth is that if you knew you could handle anything that came your way, what would you possibly have left to fear? The answer is: Nothing

I agree with her. I have heard lots of times that the best things in life happen beyond fear. Now my real question is what is the antidote to fear and how can we get that?

Keep repeating these same behaviors or strategies. After a few times, we start to predict what will happen next. In other words, we engage in generalization or inductive thinking

Be Happy

'Giving' can make a person feel happy. If you do a favor for your friend or someone else, you will often find yourself feeling happy. In the same way, kids can learn to do this same thing. At an early age, begin teaching them how to give so they can make themselves happy.

Acknowledge their mistakes. Most of the time kids and adults do not easily accept their mistakes. They are not ready to take responsibility for what's done. Taking responsibility may not feel comfortable at first, but in the long run, it will lead to greater happiness.

Chapter 14

❈ Overriding the Subconscious ❈

'I am courageous and I stand up for myself'.

What we have learned over time about the subconscious mind is that its programming is powerful. It thinks only in present time. It knows nothing about the past or the future. It can't distinguish between what's real and what's imagined. It is illogical. It stores all the data of our existence from the moment of our conception and, some would say, from our past lives. It is the gatekeeper that makes sure all of our body's functions are working properly.

The Subconscious Mind: Storage and Autopilot ■

Think of the subconscious mind as the storage room of everything that is currently not in your conscious mind. The subconscious mind stores all of your previous life experiences, your beliefs, memories, skills, all the situations you've been through, and all images you've ever seen.

The best way to understand the subconscious mind is to look at the example of a person who wants to learn how to drive a car. In the beginning, he wouldn't be able to hold a conversation with anyone while driving as he would be focusing on the different moves involved. That's because he's still using his conscious mind to drive.

The Subconscious mind: Your Autopilot! ■

A few weeks later, driving becomes a natural habit that happens automatically without needing to think about it. That person could even start using his cell phone (which is definitely not recommended) or talk to his friends and fellow passengers while driving.

This happened because the driving habit has been transferred to his subconscious mind and so the conscious mind has become free. This allows him to use it to talk even while driving.

The subconscious mind is responsible for the automatic triggering of feelings and emotions that you suddenly experience upon facing a new situation. If you were about to give a presentation, then all the feelings of fear and anxiety which you might experience are, in fact, launched and controlled by your subconscious mind.

The conscious mind is, on the other hand, responsible for logic, calculations, and all actions that are performed while you are conscious. The subconscious mind also controls other functions in your body like breathing and heartbeats.

Another good example that can help you better understand the subconscious mind is the process of breathing. Before you started reading the previous line your breathing was controlled by your subconscious.

I want you now to try and control your breathing for one minute. You will be able to do so of course. This time it will be the conscious mind that would control your breathing, but when you let go of your focus, your subconscious mind will take over again.

Programming Your Subconscious Mind

When the information about driving is stored in your subconscious mind, it's stored as a program. Think of your mind as a computer and the driving information as a software that can be run automatically whenever needed.

The same goes for lots of other activities and emotions. If someone annoyed you, the installed program of anger is going to be launched and the result will be a behavior that you may regret later.

By programming the subconscious mind with new programs you can fix many problems in your personality. Just make sure that your autopilot is capable of running your system without ruining your life or causing you any problems.

Programming your subconscious can be done through hypnosis. The subconscious mind learns by repetition and not by logic. This is why you can convince someone to believe something by repeating your argument again and again rather than using logic. For more information on this topic see chapter 16.

Rules of the Subconscious Mind

In order to best use the power of your subconscious mind, you must first know how the subconscious mind works. The subconscious mind is governed by many rules.

Learning about these rules will allow you to make the best use of your subconscious mind and bring the best out of it with the least effort. At the bottom of the article is a link that contains all the information you need to know about the rules of the subconscious mind.

Ego Defense Mechanisms

Just like your body has got its defenses against physical wounds and injuries, your subconscious mind has got its defenses against emotional shocks and wounds.

These are called ego defense mechanisms or unconscious defense mechanisms. The ego defense mechanisms' main function is to protect your well-being and to help you overcome emotional shocks.

Because of ego, overriding that subconscious programming is an ongoing process. The subconscious mind has been building these programs for a long time. So, it can take a long time to uproot the negative habits that have been developed.

Positive Affirmations Done Right

The first thing, which I already shared with you, are the affirmations. Affirmations work. The reason they don't work for some people is that they are not following the right steps.

Second, control the environment. Our environment determines how we live, how we think, and how we feel. That makes a big difference to the subconscious mind. Reading the right material, talking with the right people, and staying with the right people is what creates the right environment.

When I was working with these people, they were always complaining and blaming. What I noticed about myself is that the more I listened to them, the more aggressive and angry I felt. Even I can be influenced by other people.

These are the kind of people whom we call toxic. I was being influenced by them to the point where it started hurting my mindset. It was changing my way of thinking, and I found myself becoming very critical of other people. It was bad.

Make your environment healthy. Pick and choose carefully what is allowed into your environment.

Use visualizations

Third, use visualization techniques. The subconscious mind, as I mentioned earlier, does not know the difference between what is real and what is not. With visualization techniques, we can imagine ourselves overcoming any kind of situation. I can visualize myself as the Prime Minister of Australia right now. In reality, I am not, but I can imagine it.

Our imaginations allow us to change so many things. It allows us to change even our feelings. The real power behind imagination is of the feelings. When we imagine something and we allow ourselves to feel that way, things change.

Your thinking and emotions change. You feel confident. Your whole body changes. Your body temperature changes. There have been studies on the power of visualization.

In a study done at the University of Chicago by Dr. Biasiotto, he took a group of people and split them into three groups. He tested each group on the number of free throws they could make. Then, he had one group practice free throws for an hour each day. Another group did nothing. The third group visualized themselves making free throws.

At the end of 30 days, he tested them again. The first group improved by 24%. The second group hadn't improved at all. The third group improved by 23% even though none of them had touched the ball before the second test.

There was only 1% gap between those who actually practiced and those who just imagined it. This shows the power of the mind. Imagine what kind of improvement might have been achieved if there were a group that both practiced and visualized!

Some people say that visualization can't do anything. Visualization can do so many things. The thing is, there again, it is how you visualize that makes the difference. Practice in the wrong way, and you won't win. Visualization works the same way.

Spend 10-15 minutes every day visualizing, and it's really best if you can do it three times a day. That's powerful. People sometimes visualize once a day or once a week and then complain, "Oh, it doesn't work for me."

Visualization is akin to watching a movie of your own success. If you watch it once, you may enjoy the experience, but it doesn't become part of you. If you keep repeating that movie, you can eventually recite the lines from memory. You don't even have to watch the movie to imagine the actors and actresses playing the roles. It becomes embedded in your mind and part of who you are.

When we visualize something, we are drawing or we are installing whichever picture we want to see. The reason it takes multiple times of visualization for things to work is that each time you visualize something, you are adding a new memory to your storehouse of memories on that topic. If you've had years of negative experiences with something, like math, for example, one positive experience will not be enough to outweigh all those negative experiences you've had.

The more positive experiences you add to that memory bucket, the more likely your attitude is to be positive toward math. The more times you visualize a positive outcome, the more positive experiences you add and eventually, those positive experiences can outweigh all the negative that was in there at the beginning.

Or, imagine you draw a line with a black pen. Once you draw that line, you can't remove it or erase it. How are you going to change that? You bring another pen. You rewrite and redraw over the same line, this time with another color, such as white. Maybe the first time you go over that black line with the white color, you can still see the black through it, but the intensity has been diminished.

You go over it again with the white pen. It turns grey. You go on and becomes more like white and lesser grey. Go over it three, four, five, and ten times. What will happen? Eventually, it will become white. Visualization has that much power. Repeat, repeat, repeat, and do the same thing with affirmations. Repeat with the right intention and the right emotions. It works.

21 Days To Make a Change. Three Months To Make It Stick. ◼

It takes, on an average, 21 days of persistent, consistent effort put in every day with the right intentions and emotions to make a change. After 21 days, though, it isn't like you can quit. You have to believe in that for 21 days, and consciously you will be able to see the differences.

First three weeks are needed to get rid of the old programming. Then, after three months it will become a part of your life. Then, it will be totally installed in the subconscious mind. At that point, the change can become permanent.

Understand that the uninstallation will not 100% remove the old programming, but it will no longer affect you. If someone had a negative experience and the person is suffering right now, it's going to take three weeks of continuous effort in a positive way to change that. Further, after three months, the person will still be able to remember the incident which happened, but the effect of it is not going to impact his life.

The same thing is true about our day-to-day habits. The person will often say, "Oh, I used to do things like that, but I don't do that now." They are not going to forget that they had the habit, but the impact of that is going to be gone now.

Newer beliefs and thought patterns are easier to get rid of than older ones. They don't yet have their own imprinting in the brain. They don't have as many chances to reinforce themselves in the brain and create those neurological pathways. If it hasn't been repeated much, we can easily shake it.

But, if that new belief is related to some past experience, it will be just as hard to get rid of as the older, pre-existing beliefs. A new belief linked to older beliefs will take the same amount of time to change as the older beliefs would.

This is because when a new belief is tied to some past experience, the person has a solid reason to hold on to that belief. For example, I spoke earlier about my neighbor who is 72 years old and holds onto some negative beliefs about certain groups of people.

She had some bad experiences with this group of people. She got a new neighbor who also belonged to this group. Now, she complains all the time about that guy. He makes too much noise, he doesn't keep up with his stuff, all such kind of complaints.

Because she's having a bad experience with this new guy, she finds her old belief about that group of people reinforced. It is even harder to change her belief now, than it was earlier. It all depends on how we build a new belief as to how easy or difficult it is to change.

Accelerating The Process of Change

This is an important thing to know when trying to change your beliefs. The same principle that makes it harder to get rid of a new belief works for the new beliefs you are trying to adopt. It is important to find an older, positive belief that you can use to tie the new belief you are trying to form if you really want it to stick.

It also depends on how we pick our new beliefs, and how we associate the new beliefs with the past experiences. It will make a big difference. That has lots of power.

It is possible to change someone's beliefs in a single session. The right perspective, seen at the right moment, when the person is receptive to it can clarify things for that person to the point where s/he is able to get rid of negative beliefs and adopt new, positive beliefs.

For example, a friend of mine spent years struggling with math. She believed, and had accumulated plenty of evidence to prove it, that she was bad at math. She believed she didn't like math because she'd struggled with it for so long and for so many years. Then, a professor said one sentence to her that made all the difference in how she saw math.

He said, "Math is about relationships."

My friend did not have trouble with her relationship skills. She knew she was good at those. So, if she was good at relationships, and math was about relationships, she knew she could be good at math too. Suddenly, she believed she could learn math and be good at it.

She started to see math as a way of telling very succinct stories about relationships. As an example, the equation $-x + (x+1) = 1$. It is the story of an individual (1) who encounters something positive (x). That positive experience should have led to growth. However, something negative came along which was equal in power to the positive experience. Now, instead of growth, the individual experiences stagnated.

My friend now loves math. She understands it, whereas she didn't earlier. All she saw before was numbers, letters, and symbols. Now she sees stories and meaning.

If you hold a belief that you are not good at something, find something you are good at and find a way to relate the thing you want to become good at to that thing you already know you are good at and you have found the key to success. Any belief or anything we want to change, if we associate that thing with a positive, we can change our belief in an instant. It's a matter of finding what it is you believe and prioritize, and finding a way to connect what you want with a positive belief you already hold.

Tony Robbins states that a belief is like a table. The table has four legs. We need to break the table's legs first in order to break the belief. And he is right. We can actually break the legs to break the table of belief.

But there is another way. When someone holds a belief, rather than breaking the belief, we can change its association to something positive. This allows a person to change much faster.

Hypnosis and Reprogramming the Mind

Hypnosis is a very vast subject. It is a scientific technique and the process has the power to take a person into a state where they are willing to open their subconscious mind. It allows you to bypass the conscious and start talking directly to the subconscious. This is a matter of science. Someone can do this with self-hypnosis as well, which is a kind of meditation.

We talk each and every day with our subconscious mind. We talk about what we have done and what things are. When we talk to ourselves, we're speaking to the subconscious mind.

"No, no. I can't do this."

Why?

"Because I haven't done this before."

Hypnosis has that same power. We can go and we can explore what happened. And it is done on the basis of the scientific method. Hypnosis can actually be effective in different ways. It can empower the subconscious mind and give positive messages. Self-hypnosis is a really popular tool to empower ourselves with. It's a kind of record we can keep in the mind. Nowadays, we can buy self-hypnosis CDs.

I know about hypnosis and have done it before, but I can't say much about it. However, this is what I do know. It is a scientifically proven method by which we can help people who have negative beliefs or negative incidents which are causing them to suffer get rid of those negative thoughts. It can help the person to lead a healthy and good life.

With hypnosis, we can change someone's thinking. In hypnosis, someone is given a command. For example, "Okay, when you wake up, as soon as you see my glasses or my pen, you are going to write something on the blackboard." And they do it.

After finishing, the subject sees the pen, what is he going to do? He's going to pick up the chalk and write something on the board. I learned this technique from a very renowned hypnotherapist in India who is known for his work in clinical psychology.

He did this a couple of times in front of me. I watched him, I saw him, I read his book. When he hypnotized clients, he gave them a suggestion that as soon as they saw this, they're going to perform that act. Without any instruction, the person sees that thing and goes and does that. What this tells us is that we can give new meanings to the symbols in the subconscious mind when we hypnotize someone.

What was that? That was the reaction. They saw the pen, the person thought, "Oh, I need to write something on the board."

It is the same thing when we drive. Initially, we consistently drive with our foot hovering near the brake. After a few years, what happens? We are talking to someone, doing some other things alongside. As soon as the red light on a traffic signal comes up, we put on the brakes. What does this mean?

Our subconscious mind has learned that red means brake. The conscious mind doesn't work at that time. The subconscious mind receives the indication and it has learned that red means brake.

This is the same thing the hypnotist can do with someone else. Hypnotize the person and they can do at least that. They can change the meaning of the thing. Hypnotism has that much power. So it is really a good tool to remove some negative incident or to build a positive affirmation or cause you to think about something differently.

However, there are dangers, no doubt. The danger is that if hypnosis is not properly ended or submitted properly, it can create physical issues because there are emotional energies involved and if the emotional energies are not released properly they can get stuck there in the brain. Sometimes, people come up after finishing the hypnosis and complain about a headache because the energy is stuck somewhere. Hypnosis has lots of power and no doubt if someone is not really trained, a lot of times they don't know about this.

Hypnosis should not be treated like a parlor trick or a game. It should be done by someone who is properly trained. If it is not a scientifically proven method and the person is not trained, it's not good for them to perform that process. I strongly suggest not doing this.

However, we can do self-hypnosis. We can do that. Consciously, we can give a suggestion to the subconscious mind. How can we do that? There are different brain waves. When we are consciously aware that we are going to sleep, the person becomes relaxed and calm, at that time the person can give themselves a suggestion about what they want to change. It's like a positive affirmation.

How Perception Is Formed

I will show you a quick example. One day, and this is still so clear to me that I can actually visualize what happened, I was studying for my bachelor's in psychology. I was in the boarding school. One of my friends was in the same class. We were sitting together.

Another guy came. He was a geography student. He came there and he was making fun of us. "What are you doing? You're psychology students?" He mocked us. "Tell me a little bit more."

My friend was sitting there and he said, "Okay." There was actually a picture on the wall. He said, "What are you seeing there in that picture?"

The guy said, "Two birds and some circles."

My friend asked him, "What's the red circle?"

The guy said, "It looks like a chapati."

Chapati is a type of flatbread.

My friend said to him, "You are hungry right now."

The guy said, "Yes, I am hungry."

How we perceive things is based on what we feel right now. That is how perception works. What you feel, what you think, and what you see.

For The Subconscious, Experience Is Reality

The subconscious mind actually reacts, it doesn't respond. And when it reacts, it reacts on the basis of past experiences. So whatever happens to the subconscious mind, that's truth to it. It doesn't distinguish between truth and lies.

For the subconscious mind, whatever kind of memory or incident it is holding, that is the truth for it. What's happening right now, the subconscious mind can't differentiate.

The conscious mind has that power. The conscious mind compares what is happening right now with what happened in the past. The subconscious mind doesn't work that way. It has only its own memories, like data. The conscious mind has that power. It can differentiate.

For example, have you ever been to Delhi, the capital of India? Let's say you have not been there, and I ask you, "Do you know what Delhi looks like?"

Think of this. You've never been there. You can't describe what Delhi is like.

The same thing happens here. The person who has never seen something can't describe it. The person asking you might say, "Oh, it doesn't matter. Just tell me a little bit."

Can you tell him something?

You might be able to guess, based on a past experience with things that you know or based on your education or pictures you may have seen. You might tell me, based on what you have noticed and seen, that it probably has buildings and houses and people.

However, somebody else could come and tell you, "There are no buildings. There's a whole desert there. People don't live there." They could say that to you, right? You wouldn't know the truth. If I tell you the city is a desert, that's it, because the only thing you know about Delhi is on the basis of your education.

Suppose I said that 500 meters away from the capital, there is a place called Bhopal. I tell you the place very nice and beautiful. You're going to believe that. Meanwhile, no, there is a big chemical factory there and that is the reality.

But because I am going to tell you, "Oh, it's a nice place," you're going to believe the thing I told you until you have a personal experience to change that belief.

So, yes. On the basis of knowledge and education, what we have heard, we build our perception. So many times I have encountered such things here in Australia. When I moved here, people who had never been to India and had no clue about my country had so many negative views about it.

"India is poor. India is this. People live in slums. People are beggars there."

How do you know?

"I saw the movie, Slumdog Millionaire."

Come on, man. Slumdog Millionaire is not representative of all of India. But that's the way we build our perception. What we perceive and what we see becomes our truth until new experiences challenge that belief.

Accessing The Subconscious Mind

In addition to visualization, positive affirmations, subconscious mind suggestions given before bed, and self-hypnosis using CDs for meditation there are other tools to help you access the subconscious mind. Art, literature, and music are some very powerful tools.

Art has a really very big role to play. Drawing and painting represent your subconscious mind. Most big artists use their subconscious mind. Sigmund Freud used to do that.

As psychologists, we have this tool called the Thematic Perception Test. We show a picture to someone and ask them to write down what happened, what's happening, and what's going to happen, just about that one picture. They're going to write about that picture based on their personal experience, what they've learned, and what they've been educated to believe.

Another diagnostic tool is the Rorschach Ink Blot test. This allows us to dig into the subconscious mind by having them describe what they see when they look at the blot.

Writing is literature, and when you write something, you use your subconscious mind. Art uses the symbolic language of the subconscious mind. In other areas, like musicians or singers, they are really very famous and popular. They use what happened to them as the basis of their work.

Art and literature can work in other ways, too. Maybe you'll notice that sometimes people who are watching TV start crying. We empathize with the characters in the show. In horror movies, the same thing. We can use this same power to reprogram our brains and help us as well. When we read something and feel strongly about that, again, 93% of our subconscious works on feelings. It works very well.

There's a power in what we watch, what we read, what we see, and what we hear. It has the power to change the subconscious mind. This plays a very big role.

The subconscious mind has a lot of power. Teaching the subjects of art and literature gives kids important tools to help them shape that power. Art may represent someone's personality. It allows us to view things. It can give a visual to the innermost feelings.

Whether it is a singer, big artist, someone who plays an instrument, someone who is drawing or painting, there are so many kinds of arts, even martial arts is a kind of art that you do with your body. All these are a representation of someone's personality.

Literature is based on whatever we are reading. It is written from their personal experiences or research that can impact someone. What we read is based on experience, on our personal experiences. It impacts a person, no doubt. Whatever we do to keep repeating something, we can make it part of our subconscious mind. This happens, actually.

With literature, we pick it on the basis of interest as well, which is the impact of the personality. And the personality is shaped by the subconscious mind there, too. It is formed by how we are born and brought up. Literature has a very big impact both personally and professionally. Doctors, neurosurgeons, scientists, and engineers all need to read. I don't think there is any profession or area where reading is not important.

There's a very famous writer, who wrote Harry Potter. Her name is J.K. Rowling. How did she write that fiction? She never saw such a world.

She based her writing on her past experiences, and those experiences come from the subconscious mind.

She was going through a very hard time while she wrote. Many publishers rejected her book. They didn't think kids would like it. They rejected her book on the basis of their personal experiences. But the guy, the smart guy, who accepted the book, gave it a test. He used the conscious mind to test the experiences of the subconscious mind and see if it was true.

Visualization Before Bed

Using visualization techniques before bed is very powerful. The logic behind it is once we go to bed, most of the senses kind of settle, specifically the eyes. When you close your eyes, the rest of the senses become stronger. When we go to lie down, the brain starts working the same way. All the different brain waves start working.

What happens? Whatever we do before bed stores away in the brain and the imprint of that thing, what we've done before bed, stays longer and becomes stronger.

After that, all the other senses kind of stop working. Like I said before, every single second we get more than 60,000 bytes of data coming to us. When we go to bed, that slows down and what we have done is imprints more strongly.

Maybe people have experienced, especially kids, when they watch a movie and then they go to bed, they sometimes react in sleep. Like if it's a horror movie, they get scared.

For example, my friend when she was five years old, the movie, Earthquake, came out. It was all about a giant earthquake in California. Everybody was dying and buildings were collapsing on top of people. Her older sister didn't want her to watch the movie because she told my friend she would have nightmares. However, my friend was stubborn and determined to watch it anyway. That night, she had nightmares about buildings falling on top of her and the earth shattering beneath.

It happens that way. The same thing, though, can happen in another way as well. If something can happen and cause negative things, positive things can happen too. Whatever kind of signal you are giving to your brain before going to sleep, you are going to work on that particular information.

So, if you are going to pray, offer prayers of gratitude. Just say thanks to someone. You can do only one thing, either prayer or visualize. Or, you can use the visualization as your prayer.

Whatever you fall asleep thinking about is basically what you are telling the brain to work on while you are sleeping. It's a contradictory thing, though. It's not a hundred percent correct. The intensity of emotions determines the priority of work. So, for example, if something happened during the daytime, that's really emotional and intense, that will come up. It will overpower whatever it is you thought about before bed.

Intensity makes a big difference. If you go to bed with something and you pray or visualize or whatever you want to do, if you bring your emotions with it, it will work more. If you just visualize and see the things that are happening, it's ok. But if something is stronger emotionally than your visualization, that will come up as well.

The alpha brain wave state is very powerful for helping your conscious mind to access your subconscious mind and making your visualizations work better. This state is the one you go into right before sleep. Controlled breathing triggers that state.

"In the Alpha state, we are calmer, centered, intuitive; able to absorb, learn, and retain new information - it's ideal and feels so good! The attentive relaxation or Alpha state through effortless breathing, meditation, yoga, qigong, tai chi, prayer, relaxation exercises, and hypnosis improves the quality of each moment of our life. In alpha, our body also produces more endorphins helping dissolve the pain or inflammation." – Robert Labensart, certified hypnotherapist.

Put your hand on your abdomen so you can feel your breathing. Inhale as deeply as you can, and exhale as fully as you can. Repeat this until you feel relaxed. Continue breathing this way as you imagine the positive outcome you desire.

Writing Things Down

Something that can be done to help clear out those negative emotions before bed is to spend 30 minutes before you plan to go to bed either dumping out onto paper everything that is in your mind or in a journal. Sort these things. Whatever negative things are in there, find a way to rewrite them in a positive light.

For example, if you got fired that day, maybe it was very upsetting to you. So you write what happened. And you find something positive to say, even if it is just, "At least I won't have to work with that boss anymore," or "Now I can find a better job."

In this way, you go to sleep with positive things and positive energy. Maybe you then spend time visualizing yourself in a better job, or working for a better boss, or maybe even starting your own business instead. This turns the negative thing of the day into a positive one for the subconscious mind to work on building something positive for you.

Another thing you can do is that rather than writing down the negative stuff, write something that happened which was good. Think about those things instead.

What will happen is that you will send a positive message to your brain and it is going to be even more positive once you sleep. When you write about negative and you leave it negative, you are going to be more negative. Dumping is sometimes called recalling. When you write it, you are recalling it.

However, if something keeps going in your mind over and over again, then it is a great idea to sit down and write it down, to dump it on a paper. But if every night you first write down what happened to you that was negative, and you do not rewrite it so that it is positive, it can change your emotions in a negative way.

Leaving negatives can create issues for you. Negative emotions can disturb your sleep, create headaches for you the next morning, or other physical symptoms. Negative emotions can create lots of physical issues for you.

Before going to bed, write something positive. If you can write in your journal, that's a great thing. I do it every day. I like my journal and I write my morning pages every morning in the morning. I just write my thoughts.

Before I go to bed, I write gratitude. I don't write negative, usually. I used to tell my clients to write negative stuff. When you write the negative, especially those thoughts which are recurring, that must come out. Writing is very powerful. When you write something, it's going out of the brain. No doubt. I don't know the logic or the science behind it, but I have seen this power. When you write something, it goes out.

I've done this with myself as well about 12 years ago. It was the first time I broke up with my girlfriend. I was very attached to her. I didn't want to talk about this particular incident and what happened with me. My friends and family were very concerned. Some of my friends were worried I might be depressed, but nothing happened to me just because I was focusing on the idea as I wrote every single thing.

While I was in the relationship, I wrote every single thing. What kind of relationship we had, what was the intensity, so I wrote down every single thing, and I actually never faced any challenge. But I used to treat the people who were depressed after a relationship break up. I always advised them to bring it all out.

I used to say to them, "Go and write it down. Go and write it down, then we will talk about this."

Then we replace these with the positive. And it has power. When you raise the negative, especially a particular incident which is really disturbing, write it down. But I don't suggest you write this thing down before bed without making it into positive.

I haven't read about this and I haven't done an experiment so far as to what happens if, before we go to bed, we write negative thoughts or what happened with negative, as it changes emotions. If you are able to replace those negative emotions with positive thoughts, that's great.

Dreams and the Subconscious

According to Sigmund Freud, dreams are the royal road to the subconscious mind. Whatever we've got in our subconscious mind - history, conflicts or any other things, they come into our dreams in a symbolic form. And there are lots of studies that have been done about this.

For me, dreams are a kind of therapy. When we see the dreams, they release stress or tension in a different form. This is the thing.

According to science, we have two kinds of dreams. Content dreams and manifest dreams. Dreams sometimes come up with different things, like I can see myself somewhere and someone is with me. There is no extent of that.

But dreams can create their own stories. The subconscious mind is like that. It can mix our experiences together because it doesn't have any logic about what can be done in dreams. You may have experienced this yourself.

Dreams are symbolic. The subconscious mind only has symbols as its language. The reason there are so many questions about them is that they don't have any logical form to them. They just come up and show up that way.

They resolve lots of issues which we can't resolve consciously. Sometimes they give us indications that there's a problem we need to fix.

How you interpret dreams makes a big difference as well. When you use your logical mind you may misunderstand what the subconscious mind is trying to say. Often, when people have negative dreams, they are convinced that those events will happen because they can't decode and interpret their dreams correctly. They just take them literally and start suffering inside because of those.

Because dreams use a language of symbols, if you want to understand what a dream is saying, you can't just look at what a thing is in the dream. You have to look at what it means to you and what it does. For instance, dreaming about a house is not usually about a house at all. Think about what a house means to you. It is, for most people, a place of safety, security, and comfort. If your dream is about something coming along and destroying your house, it probably means that something has come along in your life that destroyed your sense of safety, security, and comfort.

Sometimes dreams work for us like a visualization technique. Dreams can prepare us to do something different or to practice something that is new to us. For example, you are going to move from one place to another. You keep thinking about how you are going to adjust to the new environment, the new situation, the new job, the new school or the new colleagues.

Because you keep sending messages to your subconscious mind about how you are going to do that, you may find yourself dreaming about it. Somehow, on the basis of previous or past experiences, we find the answer to that thing. Subconsciously, inside the subconscious mind, we dream about it.

In dreams, we can also start believing that we can do things that we've never done before. We subconsciously build our belief that we can do it, but consciously we are still not-confident in our ability or haven't fully mastered it yet. This is a very good sign because it builds our confidence and leads us to say, "Yes, I can do that."

Dreams can also be a source of inspiration for us. While we sleep, the subconscious uses that time to sort through the bytes of data we have collected through the day and look for connections to things we already know. Because it doesn't worry about logic, it can sometimes find unexpected connections and relationships between seemingly unrelated ideas. This is an inspiration!

Chapter 15

⇐ Beliefs and Decision Making ⇒

'Today, I abandon my old habits and take up new, more positive ones'.

While working with various people of different cultural backgrounds, I find that people often make decisions or make up their minds about something on the basis of their beliefs, especially those they built during the early stages of imprinting.

Imprinting

Dr. Morris Massey, a social scientist, calls the initial years of a child, up to the age of 7, the imprinting stages. This is where our values and sense of right and wrong are developed. That imprinting stage has been actually proven.

During this stage of development, a child absorbs everything they see, hear, smell, taste, touch, and feel. These things imprint themselves on the subconscious and determine how the children see the world around them and what they believe to be true about themselves and others.

The first imprinting stages are a very innocent phase. During this, kids are forming their beliefs. They are like melted wax that you might put your hand into. When you lift your hand, you can see the fingerprints.

Early childhood is especially important to imprinting. Whatever we learn during this stage, stays with us for a long time. This is when we form our beliefs and derive most of the meanings out of the things that happen to us. 80-90% of our beliefs form before the age of 7.

The years before age 7 are the foundation of everything. It lays the foundation of a young adult, the foundation of a young man. What we teach, how a person experiences that, what beliefs we form, and what meaning we assign to those incidents are what shape and form the rest of our lives.

The main concern of a parent during this stage should be - what experience we are giving to our kids. In that imprinting stage, if someone has a good experience and someone else has a bad/negative experience, they are going to make their beliefs on the basis of that.

When a child is in the mother's womb, they start experiencing the world at that time. What experience they have in the womb prepares them for the real world they are going to meet soon. These experiences make a big difference in their lives.

Not only their personal experiences but what they watch and learn from their surroundings, model their behavior. What kind of behavior their parents have matters because kids learn from them.

One of my friends was talking to my brother. Her brother has a daughter, and they were living in the same apartment. It was a small apartment and, sometimes, when they would yell at one another, his daughter, her niece, used to tell her granny. She would copy the way that her father and mother talked to people and to each other.

She was modeling their behavior and mimicking their voices. The three-year-old might not be able to understand, but she can model. So, it is my opinion that as an adult or as a parent, we should be very careful what experiences the kids, we care for so much, are having and what kind of exposure we are providing them. Emotional and spiritual experiences make a big difference.

Let's say you are giving your kids all the things - the cars, the toys, and all that stuff. What about the emotional attachments? Is the kid really attached to you or not? And how are you treating your kids?

I met her parents and they seemed very nice. I saw the lady twice. She has two kids and they were dressed very nicely. Her son is five or six months older than my son, but the way he was doing the activities, I was blown away.

I talked to his mother present there. She was making him independent. She would allow him to go and do things. The language she used with him was very positive. She allowed him to make his choices, just made sure it wasn't going to hurt him, and taught him how to deal with other kids.

Conversation and Interaction ■

"I am conquering my illness; I am defeating it steadily each day."

In a 2014 article featured in Psychology Today, Art Markman wrote about the development of language skills in early childhood. He cited a study by Lauren Adamson, Roger Bakeman, Deborah Deckner, and Brooke Nelson that was published in the June 2014 issue of Child Development. The study tracked a group of toddlers through their kindergarten years to see how their ability to communicate and use language evolved over time.

When the study began, each child was eighteen months old. Parents and children used primarily non-verbal communication to interact with each other. One year later, there was a lot of difference between the kids based on how much language was used while interacting with their parents. By three and a half, though, almost every child was using language in every interaction with their parents.

According to the article, "As soon as children learn to speak reasonably well, their interactions shift immediately to the use of language, because it is such an important tool for communicating."

Unhealthy Imprinting: What To Do ■

"My thoughts are filled with positivity and my life is plentiful with prosperity."

Imprinting matters, but if something went wrong during the imprinting stage, it doesn't mean we can't help that person. When they are teenagers, it is somewhat challenging for them. They need to see a professional or perhaps start building their own insights as to what they are doing is good for them, good for other people, good for the society, and good for everybody. When they put this insight along with what they are doing, and the results of their actions, then they are ready to change.

With the help of professionals, we can change their thinking. No doubt that the learning in the imprinting stage is going to impact them, but we can change that for a fact. They can change it with a conscious awareness. It will really help them a lot.

If someone is abused at an early stage, and someone understands that s/he is suffering from that abuse and don't want other people to suffer because of it, the person can stand and say they were abused. Another person may say, "Oh, I was abused." The insights and the understandings make a big difference when they see what the consequences of their actions are.

Begin with an awareness of your behavior. This can lead you to figuring out where the imprinting went wrong, so that you are able to fix it. If you are looking for professional help, the professional can help you fix that with timeline therapy and hypnotism. Self-hypnotism works as well, but conscious awareness always helps.

Consciously, we can change our unconscious behavior. Once we've decided we want to change it, we can change it. It takes some time and is a little challenging, but we can change.

Lots of people have bad habits. The habits come from the unconscious mind. Any habit can take a long time, but bad habits especially take a long time to change. It takes a long time to form a good habit, but we can do it. We can change with a conscious decision.

I noticed this with my son. When I was younger, I was a very curious guy. As a teenager, I was aggressive. My parents used to tell me I was very aggressive. But when I was in grade 10, I made a conscious decision to change. I realized my behavior wasn't good. I was hurting myself and hurting other people and I needed to change that.

I didn't go through any therapy or anything. I changed myself. It took a bit of time, but I changed myself. That conscious decision is still helping me. I learned how to deal with relationship conflicts.

When I worked with my clients going through relationship conflicts, mostly I discovered that they had bad habits. Because of the bad habits, there were big issues. I help those people, without doing any intervention, change their language and make them aware. That's it.

People often live together for a long time and never show each other appreciation. They never realize what the other person has done for them, and they don't understand why they have problems. With conscious awareness, they can change this.

Compulsive Behaviors and the Power of Belief

In an article 'The Rhyme and Reason of Rituals' by Janet Springer, she discussed a study published in the journal Neuroscience and Biobehavioral Reviews. The study looked at rituals and their relationship to OCD. They focused on the reasons why people engage in ritualistic, repetitive behaviors.

The researchers believe these behaviors evolved as a method of self-soothing during stressful situations, giving the person a feeling of being in control in an environment that is outside their control.

The belief of the individual is that if they do these rituals, they will have a good outcome. For those with OCD, however, their brains never register the signal that the ritual has been completed, so they end up being stuck in an endless repetitive loop.

As the article concludes, "Someone with OCD, with this same ritual, might become distraught if not able to perform it and might possibly develop other rituals to 'make sure' everything will be okay. For example, s/he might feel compelled to repeat, "Everything will be fine," a certain number of times to quell the <u>anxiety</u> felt until the children in question return home safely. These are two very different reactions and it's not difficult to see how the second scenario could snowball out of control and lead to hours and hours of compulsions."

Eating Disorders and Early Childhood

Science has recently found that many eating disorders are directly linked to early childhood experiences with feeding.

The eating experience provides not only sustenance but also an opportunity for learning. It affects not only children's physical growth and health but also their psychosocial and emotional development.
- Yi Hui Liu, MD MPH, Martin T. Stein, MD,
University of California, San Diego, USA

Children whose parents are excessively controlling in their approach of how, when, and what to eat can cause their children to fail to develop healthy attitudes and behaviors toward eating, which can last a lifetime.

It is important, as adults and parents, to be aware of our body's nutritional needs and to teach our children to become aware of those needs too. When those needs are neglected or ignored, it can cause serious dysfunctions toward eating later in life.

Nurturing Confidence

When I was hardly 3 years old, living in a joint family with my other cousins in the same house, there were nine of us. I was the youngest one. The oldest one was around 15 years old then. I was told that I was sharp, very determined, always moving forward, brave, and courageous.

My elder sister was very silent and lived within herself. She never talked to anyone. She just played with her toys. A cousin who was younger than her, but older than me, was naughty. He used to hurt my sister. One day, he did the same thing with me and I cried.

My parents were watching this. My father wanted to say something to him, but my mother said, "Don't say anything to his parents (meaning my uncle and aunty). They never stop him from beating my sister. Now, just wait and watch."

After a few minutes, I went back to my cousin and slapped him. He started crying.

I share this because every single child has guts. The only difference is how we nurture that.

According to my parents, I was very keen to learn new things. I always wanted to know how things worked, such as my toys, pens, clocks, and so on. As a grown adult, I can't see these traits or characters in me.

When I was in pre-school I was energetic and had leadership qualities. I was always leading my other friends into doing activities that made me happy. I was innovative and a leader. What happened to all that?

They did not match with my mother and other people's desires for me. My folks had an image in their mind of what a good kid should be and set the criteria or benchmarks for me to meet. When kids met the criteria, they were good kids and were appreciated. When those kids fulfilled their own desires and did something different, they were abused.

Every single time when our actions did not meet their rules or criteria, we were treated the same way. I still have a lot of pain in my heart while writing this. I feel vulnerable and angry although this happened to me more than 35 years ago.

This abuse totally killed my entrepreneurial drive, innovative and leadership skills, and guts. All that punishment stopped the creative energy flowing within me and my friends. I say 'stopped', but it was not just stopped, it was kind of killed.

When that flow is stopped at an early age, it becomes a problem later in life. We see lots of adults around us but mentally, many of them are still childish in their behavior, thinking, and emotions. They are not mature enough.

Healing From Past Pain

Because of a past incident or pain, a person can suffer a lot in his life, and sometimes it can even lead to mental disorders. The flow that was stopped for me was the flow of emotion to courage and that of love to compassion.

I strongly believe that most of these things are set at an early age. Your mind sets your emotions and defines them. I am not saying you can't change after that, you can change everything with your conscious awareness, with acceptance, with understanding, and by taking action. I call that a breakthrough.

What I have done so far when such thoughts start coming into my mind is to start digging into the past. Many of us start blaming our past, and after we have done all the calculations, we reach a point where we say we can't do anything better, and we move on. But for me, what we do at this stage is very crucial. It makes a big difference in our life.

Moving on itself has different meanings. One is, "Ok. What am I doing? What results am I getting? What results have I gotten that I don't mind and want to change as well? But I don't have the courage to take that risk in my life?"

Here again, we can hear the pain. Not taking the risk means the person wants to be in the safety zone

The Child Growth Movement

In modern psychology, after World War II, the child growth movement has been noticed. This has not just happened to my friends or me, it has happened with other people before me and is still going on. It seems like a cycle which has been going on for a long time now, say for centuries. It's becoming a very big problem for our future.

Today I read in the news that one Scottish MP, Michelle Thomson, revealed in the House of Commons that she was raped at the age of 14. She shared her personal story during a commons debate focused on the UN International Day for the elimination of violence against women.

During the same debate, Labour MP Tracy Bribin recounted how a man attempted to rape her when she was at university and just 20 years old.

Ms. Thomson said, "To be honest, looking back at that point I don't think I knew what rape was. It was not something that was talked about."

She added "It was mercifully quick and I remember first of all feeling surprised, then fear took over, and then horror as I realized I quite simply couldn't escape – because he was stronger than me and there was no sense even initially of any sexual desire from him, which I suppose, looking back, again I find odd."

I was talking with an IT security officer who deals on an international level. I asked him to share with me some of his childhood memories. He gave me a quick snapshot of his childhood, sharing his very happy and light moments.

According to him, his father never took any risks. He thinks there was a lack of guidance in his life. While talking with him, I noticed he had a range of moments with his father. His father never spared him from any mistake. I can see and feel when he felt proud of his dad. There was a moment when he had some trouble in school, but his father supported him 100%. He has few regrets though.

Label Changing Someone's Life ■

What I felt learned and noticed how one can put a label on someone, I understood that label can destroy a life. We should be very careful and think about the consequences.

The story goes that one day Thomas Edison came home and gave a paper to his mother. He told her, "My teacher gave me this paper and told me to only give it to my mother."

His mother's eyes were tearful as she read the letter out loud to her child: "Your son is a genius. This school is too small for him and doesn't have enough good teachers for training him. Please teach him yourself."

Many, many years later, after Edison's mother died, and he was now one of the greatest inventors of the century, he was looking through old family things. Suddenly, he saw a folded paper in the corner of a drawer in a desk.

He took it out and opened it up. On the paper was written: Your son is addled [mentally ill]. We won't let him come to school anymore.

Edison cried for hours and then later wrote in his diary: "Thomas Alva Edison was an addled child that, by a hero mother, became the genius of the century."

After Thomas Edison's school teacher called him addled or mentally ill in a letter, Edison's mother hid the letter from the young inventor and home-schooled him so that he could reach his full potential.

The Truth: ■

Thomas Edison was called "addled" by his teachers, but he wasn't ignorant of what they'd said. They'd called him that to his face. He was dyslexic, and research on that condition wouldn't begin for decades after he left the classroom. Outraged, he brought their words home to his mother, Nancy.

Nancy confronted the Reverend Engle, Thomas's teacher, but he stuck to his assessment of the child's potential. Tom was used to learning at his own pace and playing outside all day. Nancy's methods gave Tom the freedom to ask questions and to search for answers rather than memorizing things from a book and repeating them aloud, which was Reverend Engle's preferred method. Tom was struggling to adapt to the new methods.

Young Thomas also wasn't used to being whipped with a leather strap, something both Reverend and Mrs. Engle employed regularly and with vigor. Nancy withdrew her son and decided to home-school him. He briefly attended two more schools, but nearly all his childhood learning took place at home.

"My son is not backward!" declared Mrs. Edison, adding, "And I believe I ought to know. I taught children once myself!"

Later in life, Edison said, "My mother was the making of me. She was so true, so sure of me and I felt I had something to live for, someone I must not disappoint."

I hope you have read this message somewhere on the social media. It is trending very well everywhere, and it is a powerful illustration of the importance of avoiding labeling others.

Early Childhood Experiences   ■

A friend of mine has a two-year-old daughter. The family has been traveling Australia for about a year while living in a caravan. I often wonder how this experience is going to impact their little one. Every week, the child will see new places and new people. There are no kids around her, just her parents. She used to go to childcare, but not anymore.

I have no research to answer this question. However, what I do know is this - A baby's brain is very fragile. Her impression of new things is not going to stay long.

It's going to be a lot like you write something on a page and, after a couple of days, you rewrite something on that same page. The memories are not going to consolidate. This exposure might give her scrambled and vague memories in the future.

My second question is - how the impression of memories will work for her. If memory imprints are like putting a hand in warm wax, before it gets cold or consolidates, and we put another hand on that same impression, now there are two imprints. Which one can you really see?

Motivating Your Child

I have heard lots of times that a person needs more motivation to get success in his/her project and in another talk about how s/he is highly motivated to do that thing.

If we look into studies and theories of motivation, which may be hundreds in number, my main concern remains to dig more into how one can get motivated and how it works. Maybe you've heard lots of success, heroic stories or journeys.

I read about the author Tony Robbins, one of the best personal development coaches in the world. He had a very challenging childhood. Oprah Winfrey also had an abusive childhood. What made them so successful in their lives? What was their driving force to become a successful person? They gave back a lot to their communities as well.

As I know, your values are the real factor.

Motivation stays for a moment. Inspiration stays longer, and that is based on your personal values.

Values and Motivation

Values and Motivation are totally different. Motivation is for a moment and doesn't last long. With motivation, we can motivate anybody at any time and with anything. We can motivate anybody for a moment. But that will only last for a very limited time.

People fool themselves. They go to see a motivational speaker and expect a big change to come to their lives, but that motivation doesn't last. In sports, the same thing happens. Coaches motivate their players. They may use negative language to fire them up and make them angry, especially in boxing. That's one way to motivate.

Values stay longer. If someone has values, those are going to stay for life. When there is a value, there is no need to motivate the person to do certain things or take certain kinds of actions.

For example, during wars, the commanders used to motivate the soldiers by reminding them of their values. We are fighting for our nation or for this or that. When we motivate using values – protecting our families or parents or nation – it stays longer.

I focus on this because parents need to see what kind of values they are teaching their children. For example, there was a lawyer in a court. He received an information that his wife had died. He stayed back at the court and finished his trial before leaving for his house. His main value was clearly to his profession to help other people. He did not back off even in a difficult time.

How we behave teaches our kids what is of real value and what is not. It is what a person values for him/herself first that determines what s/he does.

A person who does not value him/herself becomes a people pleaser because the value of 'self' does not come before others. That is the main issue. According to a study done in the 80's, the majority of people don't really value themselves.

Because people don't know their own value, or if they question it, they self-sabotage and are not disciplined. They don't know how to manage their time because they do not believe they are valuable.

Motivation doesn't work that way. I can motivate someone to do something for 10 minutes. But if you don't have value in that thing, you are not going to do it for a longer duration.

My wife is a good example. She is the kind of lady who, whatever she says she is going to do, doesn't care about anything after that. She even stops sleeping and eating because she values other things more. That's because she values her commitment and herself more than sleeping and eating. And that's why she does that.

I know plenty of people who tell you, "I'll call you or I'll see you on this date," and then they never show up. They do not value themselves nor do they value their own or others' time. This is the difference between value and time.

For kids, we can motivate them, "Oh, you can do this. You can go and do it." Suppose they are in the sports, "You are a superstar." I just came from childcare, and one kid tells me, "I am a superhero!"

Okay, that's good. You're a superhero. What's that? Superhero is just a motivation. It's not a value. The value for what? The value makes a big difference.

There are different kinds of values. There are shallow values and good values. Shadow values are a part of your ego.

My main focus is on the kids and how to help them instill good values. Those good values can be installed in them through role modeling and helping them find their passion. Language is also very important in this. What kind of language we are using with our kids. We can develop their values in that way. Language. Modeling. Teaching. This is how we can help kids develop healthy, strong values.

False Hope and Real Hope

I was playing with my son some time ago and he asked me to cry, so I did enact the drama. He said to me, "Don't worry, Mummy coming soon."

I thought to myself, "Where did he learn this thing?"

I spoke to my wife and came to find out that he learned this from his childcare. It made me wonder what we are teaching our kids. Why are we teaching them false hopes? This false hope is going to damage their trust with others and with themselves. I know that some of you are wondering what's wrong with it.

False Hope

"Momma's coming soon." What's this? You're giving a hope to the child, to the kid, that Momma's coming soon, and then everything will be alright. In this case, how are you giving them that feeling of hope? Maybe Momma's not coming for the next two days or the next two hours. Is it good that the kid should keep hoping, "Momma's coming soon, momma's coming soon?"

What kind of skills are you teaching the kids with this to comfort them? You're creating this hope that someone will come and save them and they can relax now. For whatever problem you're having with the baby, the solution is Momma. Is that the correct teaching for a baby?

Stay there. Momma will come help you if you wait long enough. This is teaching them learned helplessness, that they can't comfort themselves but need to wait for someone else to solve the problems for them.

My mentor always says, "Hope. Wish. Wait. These are the three things that kill people's development."

These are the three things that stop people from growing.

I hope it will get better. What are you doing to make it better? That's a hope but where's the action? Wait for something. Wait means what?

You're not taking any action. A wish is similar - no action. You wish for something, but you aren't taking any action to get it.

These three things have no action in them. False hope is hope with no action behind it, not even a plan to take any action. You're just waiting for something to happen to you instead of doing what must be done to make it happen.

You're treating life like magic as if things are just going to happen automatically. This is not a good thing to teach kids, nor is it a good thing for them to learn. It's not a resourceful way of handling the situation because it doesn't teach you how to be resourceful, it just teaches you to wait for someone else to come and solve the problem for you. They are learning helplessness.

They start depending on things and people, thinking there is no need for them to take action. They are becoming dependent on things and people outside their own control to solve their problems. How can they grow then? If they are always waiting for someone else to solve their problems, or for something to happen which will solve it, how are they going to grow?

This is what we are teaching them. Hope. Wait. Wish. These three words are killing the whole society according to my thinking. For so many people, if something goes wrong in their life, they say to themselves, "I hope it will get better." They make no plan and take no action to make it better. The hope is really good, but what are you doing right now to make it better?

Hope without action is pointless. Without action, it is just a false hope that will lead to disappointment. It is not helping people. These words are not helping anyone. And we learn such things at the beginning of our lives when we are still imprinting. When we are growing and starting to learn, we are being taught these things. These are reinforced in us again and again, and then, that's how we become and teach the same to our children.

They demotivate us, hold us back, and keep us from doing the things to improve our lives. It's not like we can just wait 10 years and then a massive change will happen. It's not going to happen that way.

For example, while I was working on getting this book finished, I couldn't just say, "Oh, if I wait 10 minutes, the book will be finished." It would not ever have happened until I put my behind in the chair and took the action of writing it.

False hope says, "I will wait for something to happen." Real hope creates a plan to make it happen and then acts on that plan.

Real Hope

No doubt, learning to wait for things is good. Developing patience is good. Kids need to learn delayed gratification. And this must be built up. With patience, you condition them with what? Hope. But it must be a real hope and not false hope.

They plant the seed and they must wait for the seed to grow. That hope that the seed will grow is based on the knowledge of how plants grow. It's rooted in facts and truth. They can't hurry the plant along. It will grow when it grows. That waiting brings patience.

I argue with my son, I know him, I made him very stubborn intentionally. He makes me crazy sometimes, he is that stubborn. When he wants something and I tell him, "No," he cries. I still say, "No." He cries louder and louder. I don't react and I don't give in. I just sit with him. That's it. Within 2-3 minutes, he relaxes. I tell him, "Just wait 2-3 minutes more." Here I am building patience.

This is a good way to break them of needing instant gratification. When they must wait for results. After the action, wait for the results.

Gardening and cooking are two very good things to do with kids to help them learn delayed gratification. Cookies take as long as they take to cook. Seeds take as long as they take to grow. You must first do the action to get the results. You can't just buy the ingredients and hope for cookies or buy the seed packet and just sit and hope for the fruit to eat. You must take the actions of putting the ingredients together, putting the cookies on the tray and then into the oven. You must take the action of planting the seeds and watering them regularly.

The waiting, though, can't be separated from the initial action. Hope without action won't produce any results. Doing nothing and expecting to get the results you want is kind of crazy. It's like expecting to win the lottery when you haven't even bought the ticket.

Sandwich Feedback

Reward and punishment are tools which parents have used for a long time to help instill habits in their children. The reward can be tangible or emotional. We call this feedback.

When the behavior is good, the parents give a reward. When it is not good, the parents give a punishment.

I was in a seminar and the speaker shared a few incidents from his personal life. One of them was about his educational journey. He said he was very good in school, getting good grades until he was fourteen.

That year, he started playing sports and his grades dropped. His father got upset and punished him with a stick. He stopped playing games and went back to his studies. Even today, although he is now forty plus, he still remembers the whole scenario that happened to him.

Authenticity

I clearly remember a story people tell in different parts of India. It illustrates an Indian philosophy. There was a lady whose son had a sweet tooth. He just couldn't resist sweets and his mother was really worried about his health. She tried so many things to help him get rid of that bad habit, but everything was in vain.

One day someone told her, "There is a Yogi at some distance who can help your son." She decided to go and see him. She went there with her son and explained her issue to the Yogi. She asked for help, but the Yogi didn't give her any satisfactory answers. He asked her to come again after two weeks. She was surprised and a bit disappointed.

She went back after two weeks and the Yogi met them and had a chat with both of them. The Yogi said one sentence, "Son, don't eat sugar anymore," and then he was done. The lady was shocked and a little angry.

"Why did you tell us to come back after two weeks? You could have said the same line two weeks ago!"
The Yogi replied, "A that time, I used to eat sugar. First, I quit that habit. Now, I have been living a sugar-free life since then. I can't tell your son to quit that bad habit if I am not willing to do what I am asking him to do. It's never going to be authentic."

Empathy

Case histories of Milton Erickson, a famous American psychiatrist and hypnotherapist famous for his instant cures, illustrate the importance of empathy. One is about a child who was very stubborn. The parents said they tried everything with him but he would throw tantrums in public places, such as the supermarket and so on, and they felt helpless to stop him. Unless they fulfilled his demands, he would lay on the floor or the ground, kicking and screaming.

Milton went with the family to a public place. The child threw his usual tantrum when he didn't get his way. Instead of reacting negatively, as the child's parents usually did, Milton lay on the ground with him kicking and throwing his own tantrum. The child was so shocked by the adult behavior that he stopped his tantrum immediately.

In another case, a beautiful 12-year-old girl named Ruth was brought to his ward. She was prone to tantrums that included stomping on people's feet, breaking their toes, kicking people in the shins, tearing their dresses, and other terrible behavior.

One day, Erickson got a call notifying him she was at it again and went to visit her. Rather than stopping her, he joined her. He then went out into the hall and ripped the dress from a nurse who had agreed to this in advance. Ruth was so shocked that she grabbed a bedsheet and wrapped the nurse in it, scolding Erickson and telling him he ought not to do such things. She wasn't a problem after that. She'd seen the ugliness of her own behavior reflected at her.

Bullying: Bullies, who often have low self-esteem, find ways to threaten.

Chapter 16

⟽ Reprogramming the Subconscious ⟾

" I have endless creativity"

To begin with, as stated in chapter 14, you must know the rules of reprogramming the subconscious mind.

Rule #1: Know what you want ■
When it comes to making a change at the subconscious level, you MUST decide what exactly you want to improve.

You have to be specific, yet not too specific. You have to be rational in your request (willing yourself to fly like a bird is not rational, but you can make it rational if you want to take a skydiving course) and you MUST focus on that, and that only!

Focusing on different subjects simultaneously can only confuse your subconscious mind; you'll be scattered and that is the opposite of being goal-oriented.

For example, if you wish to <u>find your soul mate</u>, focus on that, and don't stretch it into other areas like <u>making more money</u>, <u>losing weight</u>, and <u>overcoming anxiety</u>.

It's great to have different goals, but you have to put your focus on one at a time.

However, some goals don't require subconscious mind reprogramming at all so you can still have your main goal plus other goals that require nothing but practice (like getting a driver's license.)

If you have several goals that demand a change in the subconscious mind, choose one that is your priority.

Rule #2: Reveal the subconscious patterns that stop you ■

When you choose your main goal, you need to have a dialog with yourself and find related subconscious mind obstacles that are part of the whole picture.

For instance, a woman who wants to find her perfect partner, she needs to talk to herself, honestly, without masks, without excuses about what is stopping her from meeting the right person.

Maybe she is too dependent and that makes potential partners go away, so she needs to take care of that issue too, along with her main goal.

When you are having a dialog with yourselves, you must ask yourself:

what is preventing me from getting x? What possible blockages do I hold at the subconscious level?

Sometimes you won't be able to find the answer yourself, so you will need to get help in order to find it. The help can be a therapist or even close friends who know you the best. You must be willing to be exposed to the answer they give you.

The Reason That You Are Subconsciously Blocked Must Be Revealed ■

Let's examine another example to make this point clearer: A man is struggling to make more money, but he can't make it; something is pushing him back and it happens all the time.

He decides to communicate with his subconscious mind, but he must find the reason or reasons that he is being stopped from reaching his goal.

This could be subconscious, self-limiting beliefs such as, "Money will make me lose my family time," or it could be a behavior pattern such as the lack of perseverance and starting new projects over and over again.

He must find the cause(s), and accordingly, build a communication system with the subconscious mind.

Rule #3: Apply the subconscious shifting methods before sleep ■

When using the techniques to program the subconscious mind that are mentioned below, it must be done before sleeping time or right when you wake up in the morning.

About 15 minutes before falling asleep, the mind and body begin to calm down, the muscles loosen up, the breathing becomes more at ease, the heartbeats start to slow down, and the whole system gets into a deeper relaxation mode. At this point, the brain produces alpha waves.

Researcher's EEG studies show that in this 15-minute window between wakefulness and sleep, the brain waves slow down and there are between 7-14 electrical waves each second – those are alpha waves.

In this stage, according to the research, the subconscious mind's tunnel is 'open' to receive messages.

Talking To The Subconscious

Besides using Subliminal Messages (a complete technique that is extensively <u>detailed here</u>), there are 4 powerful ways to communicate effectively with your subconscious mind and input positive and affirmative new beliefs.

By talking directly to your unconscious brain, you will accomplish the goals you set, experience good feelings, become emotionally balanced, and feel more relaxed and at ease.

Practice today and start getting results!

Method #1 – Using Metaphors to Program Your Subconscious Mind

Metaphors have been proven to be extremely effective. They have a huge impact on your subconscious mind. No wonder so many books, plays, movies, and even commercials have been using metaphors to convey the messages.

For example, the metaphors can be a field and seeds, or a world with endless possibilities, powerful, like planes in the sky, a stable, a big tree planted on a riverside, a certain home that makes you feel comfortable, etc.

How to use metaphors to re-wire your subconscious mind?

First step – use music

Relaxing, calm, soft, and pleasant music helps the brain let go and relax. The music must be heard repetitively (every night) and it must relax you.

Avoid using music that keeps you awake and alert.

We recommend using <u>alpha brain wave music</u> that will make your brain sync with the alpha waves. Once the brain is in its Alpha state, it becomes very simple to program the subconscious mind.

The alpha brain waves tune your brain into its receptive mode. That is the reason the biggest meditation gurus around the world get into the Alpha state in order to meditate.

Second step - plant the seeds

After getting in the position of deep relaxation, this is the time to communicate with your subconscious mind. Begin to plant new messages – messages that push you toward success and progression.

At first, it might be strange and feel unnatural to you, but don't worry. This takes time and practice. Remember that your subconscious mind doesn't distinguish between reality and imagination. When the alpha waves open the gate for affirmative suggestions, powerful metaphors will do the work. Some people tend to be more rational and imaginative, the metaphorical method doesn't really apply to them.

How Can I Know If This Subconscious Mind Programming Technique Fits Me?

The method is right for you if you tend to daydream;

If you like art and have an artistic personality;

If you use metaphors in your daily life when you tell stories or talk to friends;

If you think about life as a parable having a moral;

And if you read this paragraph and liked the sound of the metaphor method.

Method #2 – Final Result

This method to <u>shift your subconscious mind</u> requires a few steps. Before starting to apply the steps below, you need to get into a comforting relaxation mode.

Two effective ways to dive into an immediate calming position

1. As mentioned in method #1 – produce alpha brain waves. You can enter into alpha brain waves easily by listening to Brainwave Entrainment Technology.
2. The second way to enter into the relaxation zone is breathing. Of course, everybody knows how to do it, but only a few know *how to do it right*. The correct way to breathe is very simple and requires only awareness.

How can I breathe right and relax immediately:

1. Inhale through your nose and take a deep breath for 3 seconds. Let the air go deeper than your lungs – feel it in your stomach (if you

do it right, you can actually see and feel your stomach expand). Fill your lower stomach with lots of oxygen.
2. Feel the air in your stomach, then feel it go up to your lungs.
3. After you feel the air in your lungs, blow it out for 5 seconds through your mouth.
4. Repeat the breathing process until you feel relaxed and calm. For experienced people, it might take only 3 sessions of breathing, while for others it might take a few more.

Remember that no matter how long it takes you, breathing correctly is extremely healthy and a natural remedy for stress relief. You can also combine the relaxing breathing process with the alpha brain wave music that was mentioned above.

The Five Steps To Program The Subconscious Mind

Choose a goal
The goal can be big or small – it doesn't matter, as long as you deeply desire it.

Imagine the result
Create the desired image in your mind and imagine how your life is going to look when it happens; visualize the final result AFTER you fulfill your wish.

Focus on how it feels
Pay attention to all the different angles – how it makes you feel, what colors you see, sounds you hear, people who are around you, where you are, what the view is around you, and how it feels to realize that you accomplished your aspiration. So, step three is video visualization and it's very effective in the subconscious mind programming process.

Static picture
You're looking at YOUR picture in the future after you achieved what you wanted – the way you want it to be. This step is static visualization – look at your life after the goal was accomplished. What's in the picture, is it framed, who are you with, does this picture have colors, and where are you? Get as detailed as possible.

Mix and match

Mix the video and static images back and forth as quickly as possible. Imagine yourself in a framed picture exactly the way you desire, then immediately switch it to motion images. Do it for 2-3 minutes. If you can last longer, feel free to do so to maximize your results and shift your subconscious mind settings faster.

* Repeat this process each night right before falling asleep for at least 21 days. It should take only a few minutes *

Guided Meditation For Subconscious Mind Programming

Many people feel that guided meditation is way more effective to create subconscious mind changes because they can really drift into it without the need to focus all the time.

BUT, if you feel you don't need assistance, do it yourself. Either way works excellently as long as you practice on a daily basis (or should we say nightly basis).

Practice Your Breathing Skills

During the day, find time at least once a day to breathe deeply.

It will help you greatly in two ways:

1. Your body will become acquainted with the right way of breathing,
2. You'll feel so relaxed and serene for the whole day, or for at least, a part of it.

All it takes is 2-3 minutes. When you practice during the day as well, it will be very easy to get into an immediate relaxation at night when you apply this breathing technique.

Method #3 – Using Past Memories to Unleash the Power of The Subconscious Mind

Like the other methods, this one also requires a calm state of mind.

Take deep breaths as explained in method 2 and get into a relaxed state of mind.

Step one: Bring to the surface a past memory

Ask your subconscious mind to bring up a good memory from the past. Most likely, many memories will pop up. Easily skip and release the <u>negative ones,</u> don't stress out about them and just focus on the good ones.

Choose only one memory

Get into it. Relive this memory all over again. If you feel this is impossible, just think about eating a lemon right now. If you can imagine yourself eating a lemon and experience the taste in your mouth, it goes the same with a past memory.

Reminiscing a positive past memory will create a good feeling instantly and will connect you with your subconscious mind.

Every night is a gift

So many people go to sleep when they think about what's wrong in their lives, who made them angry or sad... Before sleep, they're reviewing all the bad things which happened that day, that week, or in the past. These patterns have <u>damaging influences on the subconscious mind</u> if repeated regularly.

Instead of taking advantage of this great time frame opportunity to access their unconscious mind to create a profound change, they're drawn into darkness and negativity. Then they keep wondering why nothing is changing or why things turn out to be even worse.

Don't waste your precious sleeping time feeling anxious and fearful. See it as a window to make things better.

Imagine when you turn this practice into a routine, night after night, you bombard your subconscious mind with positive past images and memories. Do you think you'll be more or less anxious?

Step two: countdown

After focusing on a good memory and living this memory again, count back slowly from 100.

After every few numbers you're counting back, tell yourself, "I feel good about myself," "I love myself," "I become more and more relaxed."

You can choose different suggestions, as long as you <u>relate</u> to them and they <u>are formulated correctly</u>.

For instance, if your goal is to guide your subconscious mind to find your soulmate, tell yourself after every few moments of counting back messages, "I am attracting the perfect relationship into my life," "Love is all around me," "The universe is sending me the love of my life," "My life is full and I choose to share it with a person I love."

If you have a challenge or dilemma, just ask your subconscious for ideas on how to deal with it and tell yourself that you trust in yourself completely.

Take advantage of the night time to make a change

You are given an amazing opportunity for something great to happen.

And it's happening every night before you go to sleep.

Every night it's your chance to plant positive ideas.

It doesn't matter if you have to wake up in 4 hours. Avoid falling into excuses. Just do it!

Remember that true winners don't always do what they want, they do what's needed.

If you don't have 10 minutes to imagine a desired picture of you, using metaphors or breath, the least you can do is sync your brain with <u>alpha waves</u> to encourage your mind to calm down.

Listening to music does not require any effort, so you can easily make it every night, even if you have only a few hours to sleep.

Method #4 – Peak Moment As An Anchor to Harness the Subconscious Mind

Here's a powerful technique to program your subconscious mind that will create a new and long-lasting neuronal wiring if you use it correctly for at least 30 days in a row, every night (no exceptions).

Studies have found that it takes between 4 weeks – 90 days to create a new neural pathway in the brain.

First, choose one affirmation that fits you the most

Take your list of affirmations and choose a positive one that you want to have in your life. It could be money, a personal trait you currently don't have and you wish to implement it in your personality, or ANYTHING you wish.

If you don't have a list, it's time to make one. It is necessary because you need to know what you want for yourself, your life, where you are going, what your direction is, and what your goal is.

The affirmations need to be formulated in a specific way in order for them to be effective, if you don't know how to do it.

After you choose a thought you relate to the most and determine that you desire to implement it in your subconscious mind, you can now move forward to the second step.

Second, remember an event that made you feel an extreme excitement

Focus on an event or situation that made you feel that you were on the top of the world. It could be anything – your first date, your first sale in your business, when you asked out someone you had a crush on for a while and this person said 'yes', when you won a soccer game, or when you made a successful move in poker and won the whole pot.

It can be any memory that was very significant for you and that made you FEEL bursts of positive emotions.

Maybe it will be a little difficult to find something like that because your mind is not used to going back to happy memories. Most people's subconscious minds are completely programmed to go back to sad memories and experience them over and over again. Take your time and remember an event you participated in that made you feel an immense excitement.

Third, Get into that event with full power

You chose one? Great! Now the **next step** it to remember it again, with all the details of how you FELT.

Try to reminisce about how happy you were, the smells, colors, sounds, your heartbeats, your smiles, the view around you, how people reacted to you, and what you were doing that caused you this enormous excitement.

Feel the sense of the flow, get deeply into it, and be there again in your subconscious mind, no matter how long it takes you to get there.

Once you dive in and are re-experiencing these powerful and positive emotions, <u>it is the PERFECT time to connect it to the affirmation you want to achieve the most.</u>

An example of a powerful past event

For example, imagine yourself in college, giving a presentation in front of your whole class; 50 people are staring at you and waiting to see what you have to say.

You're starting to talk and you're a little bit scared; then you get into it pretty easily and the speech starts to flow. Suddenly you remember all you need to say.

You get <u>confident</u> on the classroom stage and feel you own the crowd. You feel you have conquered your fear of public speaking; you begin to realize you just LOVE this feeling that people are listening to you and you're enjoying talking to them loudly, with confidence.

You FEEL so proud of yourself and the fact that you're actually doing it, standing right there, looking in people's eyes. You FEEL this is actually very easy, fun, and enjoyable to be there and experience it.

You feel you just discovered a new world of comfort in front of other people and you would like to give speeches again and again, and again…

THEN, at the point that you feel this massive excitement, it's time to implant the affirmation you want to have the MOST.

Why is this subconscious mind technique so powerful?

When an event (a real or imaginary one) stimulates a gigantic sense of excitement within you, a protein is released along with the neurotransmitters, when the impulses cross the Synaptic Cleft.

This action causes this event to connect to the neurotransmission (i.e. synaptic transmission) in a much more intense way than just a regular memory which doesn't carry any emotion.

When you are reminiscing about this event and re-experiencing it and bringing back those emotions from the past, another protein releases. And when you attach the affirmation to this event, you are physically linking this affirmation to the existing neurotransmission.

Notes To Make The Most Out Of The Subconscious Mind Programming Process

1. Focus on ONE affirmation for a period of at least 4 weeks.
2. Do it every night before sleep or just when you wake up
3. Get into a routine – create neuronal wiring in the same place and time. If you're used to reflecting and evoking emotions at 9:00 pm, do it every night at around the same time.
4. Find 5-10 minutes during the day to repeat it. If you think you don't have time, give up watching TV, or something else you're used to doing that is unnecessary. Creating a new neuronal pathway and shaping your new reality is more important than a TV show.

Pick One Or Use Them All – Your Choice

Each of the four subconscious mind programming techniques listed above is a great way to communicate with your subconscious mind, to program it, and to remove the obstacles and limiting beliefs you have. Choose the one that works best for you.

It's absolutely possible to use all four of them each time to access to the full power of the subconscious mind, but one of the most important keys to success in this process is persistence.

Of course, you must do it right in addition to being persistent: avoid getting sucked into negative thoughts, be goal oriented and focus on your desires in these exercises.

It only takes a few minutes a day.

Addendum: Imagery Basic Relaxation Script

By Martin L. Rossman, MD

I'm here to offer you a simple way to use your mind and your imagination to create for yourself a state of mind that's peaceful, pleasant, relaxing, restful, and refreshing. Really, what I'm going to invite you to do is to have a daydream.

Daydream yourself to a place that's very beautiful to you, very peaceful, and very safe. Begin by paying attention to your breathing, and let yourself take a few nice, deep, full breaths. Let yourself breathe into your abdomen, bringing your breath all the way down into your belly, and allowing your out-breath to be a real letting-go kind of a breath. As if with that breath, you can begin to release any tension, or discomfort, or distraction that you don't need to hold on to. You're just using that breath to begin shifting your attention from the outer world to your inner world and to take a five-minute break and go to a place that's peaceful and beautiful. And induce a state of peacefulness and relaxation centered within you. Let yourself imagine that when you breathe in, you're breathing in fresh energy and oxygen that's flowing through your whole body – because you are. And imagine that with every out-breath you just let go of a little bit of tension, a little bit of discomfort, a little distraction. So, you're breathing in energy and relaxation, and you're letting the out-breath be a real letting go of tension.

And you may want to allow your eyes to close because it's easier to pay attention to your inner world that way. Let any outside sounds around you be in the background of your awareness. They're not important to your purpose right now. If there ever is something you need to pay attention to, you're able to open your eyes and do that.

But begin now to imagine yourself going to a place that's very beautiful to you...very peaceful...very safe and secure — a place that you feel really good to be at. And this might be a place that you've actually been to in your life, or it may be a place you've visited before in your imagination. Or it can be a new place, some combination, or some place that you've never imagined yourself going to before. It doesn't really matter. As long as the place you're imagining is very beautiful to you...very peaceful...very safe. A nice place to be for a few minutes.

Allow yourself to imagine going there as best you can in your own way. And look around and notice what you imagine seeing in this special, quiet, peaceful place. Notice the colors and the shapes and the things that you see there. And by the way, if there's more than one place that comes to mind, simply pick the one that interests you the most right now. You can visit others at another time.

And so as you notice what you see, notice if you imagine hearing any sounds in this special, peaceful, quiet place. Or whether it's just very quiet. You may even imagine an aroma, an odor, or a fragrance in this place. And you may not. It doesn't really matter. Just notice whether there's an aroma or fragrance in the air. Notice the temperature and the time of day and the season of the year. Notice whether it's very quiet or if there are things that are alive around you. And especially notice any feelings any peacefulness, or relaxation, or comfort that you feel. And allow them to be there. And allow yourself to relax into them and to feel that relaxation, that peacefulness. Nothing else to do right now and nowhere else to go. Simply enjoying a few quiet moments in this very beautiful and peaceful place. Find the spot where you feel most comfortable and allow yourself to get settled there. Simply enjoy a few quiet moments. Peaceful, relaxed, nothing to do, nowhere to go, enjoying the beauty and the safety. As you deeply relax in this place of beauty, peacefulness, and safety, you can allow your body to recharge and your mind as well – even your spirit. Just drawing from this sense of deep restfulness and comfort that's here.

And if this is a pleasant experience, you should know that you can come back here and enjoy this anytime of your own choosing, simply by deciding to shift your attention to your inner world, allowing your breathing to get deep and comfortable, and imagining yourself coming to this very beautiful, very peaceful, very quiet place. If your mind should wander or get distracted, simply take another breath or two and refocus your mind back into this beautiful, peaceful, and quiet place and let this be your focus of attention for five minutes, or ten minutes, or twenty minutes – whatever period of time is right for you. And then when you decide to bring your attention back to the outer world, as I'll invite you to do now, allow the images to fade but bring back with you any sense of relaxation, peacefulness, refreshment — a good feeling that comes from taking a little time to find that place of calm, quiet, and peacefulness within you. And know that you can come back and visit this place anytime you choose. Also know that this place is always within you, and that by even remembering it or thinking about it, you can touch into that feeling of calmness, peacefulness, and serenity and bring those qualities more and more into your daily life.

Rossman, M. (2016). Imagery: Basic Relaxation Script. *Psych Central*. Retrieved on April 14, 2017, from https://psychcentral.com/lib/imagery-basic-relaxation-script/

About the Author

Hamesh Yadav is a behaviour expert, and from the last 24 years, he is studying and working on human behaviour. He is very passionate about this subject. He did his bachelors (honours) and masters in psychology, and Masters in Philosophy (M.Phil.) in clinical psychology. He has published various national and international academic papers. Before moving to Australia, he worked as a clinical psychologist in different hospitals and in ICMR, one of the premier institutes of India. He is a family man, father of a young child and working very close to the community and is always ready to help others. Now, he runs his coaching and training business under the name of Royal Life Coaching and assists the people to grow in their personal life and business life. He understands human behaviour codes and knows how to decode them.

www.ingramcontent.com/pod-product-compliance
Lightning Source LLC
Chambersburg PA
CBHW022130150726
47992CB00002B/524